WHAT A GREAT IDEA!

INVENTIONS THAT CHANGED THE WORLD

STEPHEN M. TOMECEK

illustrated by Dan Stuckenschneider

SCHOLASTIC NONFICTION

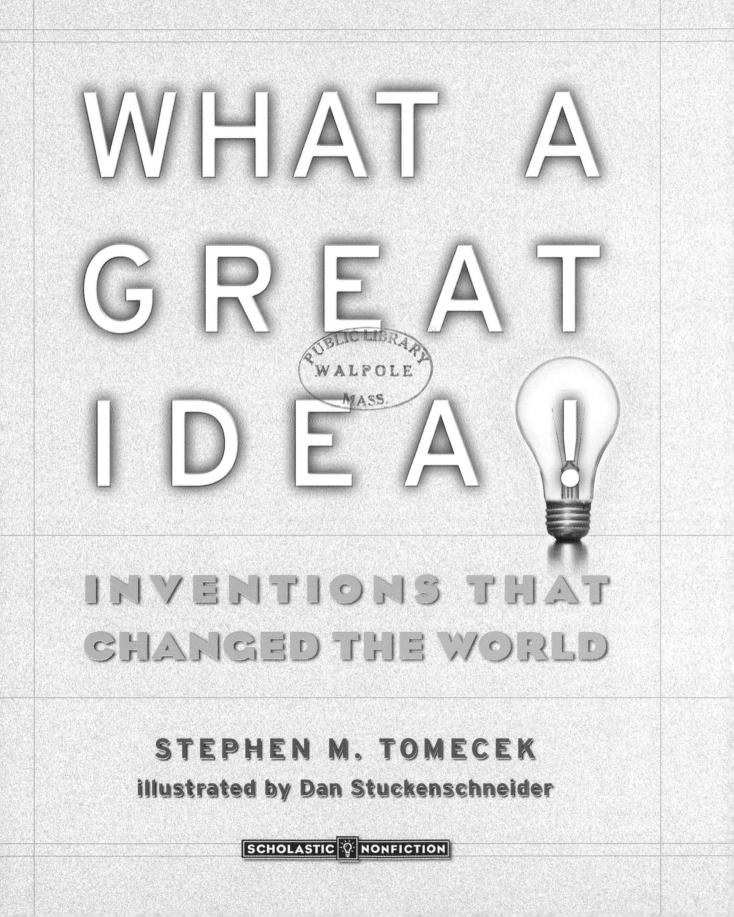

Text copyright © 2003 by
Stephen M. Tomecek ✳ Illustrations copyright
© 2003 by Dan Stuckenschneider / UHL Studios

LIBRARY OF CONGRESS CATALOGING-IN-PUBLICATION DATA
Tomecek, Stephen M. ✳ What a great idea!: inventions that changed
the world / by Stephen M. Tomecek. ✳ p.   cm. ✳ Includes index,
bibliography, Web sites, and contests. ✳ ISBN 0-590-68144-3 ✳
1. Inventions—History—Juvenile literature. [1. Inventions—
History.] I. Title. ✳ T15.T695 2002 ✳ 609—dc21
2001020937

10 9 8 7 6 5 4 3   03 04 05 06 07

PRINTED IN THE
UNITED STATES OF AMERICA
First edition, February 2003

The text is set in Century Book and the
display type is set in Interstate.
The illustrations were created in
mixed media and Photoshop.

. . . .

Book design and composition
by Nancy Sabato
Additional composition
by Brad Walrod

. . . .
▼▼▼▼▼▼▼▼▼▼▼▼▼▼▼

ACKNOWLEDGMENTS

I wish to thank the following individuals and organizations for providing inspiration and information for this book:
✳ My parents, Anna and John Tomecek, who taught me to appreciate the importance of learning from history and using it as a foundation for the future
✳ The publishers of *Invention and Technology* magazine, which helps keep the memories of past inventors alive for future generations
✳ My friend and mentor, Dr. John Loret, Director of the Science Museum of Long Island, without whose support and direction it would have been impossible for me to make the "connections" in this book

Finally, I would like to thank several people at Scholastic: My original editor, Nancy Laties Feresten, for "buying into" the concept and my current editor, Kate Waters, for helping me mold it; art director Nancy Sabato for her design; and Dan Stuckenschneider for the wonderful illustrations that make this book complete.

The original concept for this book was inspired by *Connections*, the book and television series by James Burke.

**FOR GLENN
AND SCOTT,**

two great friends

who helped me

invent a new life

✳

CONTENTS

Introduction   7

chapter one

THE ANCIENT WORLD (BEFORE 3500 B.C.)   8
The Hand Ax   10
The Spear   12
Art   14
Farming   16
Cities   18
Clothing   20
Pottery   22
Rafts, Dugouts, and Boats   24
The Axle   26

chapter two

THE METAL AGE (3500 B.C.-A.D. 1)   28
Writing   30
Mathematics   32
Measurement   34
Money   36
Metallurgy and Smelting   38
Irrigation   40
Waterwheels   42
Maps   44

chapter three

THE AGE OF DISCOVERY (A.D. 1-1799)   46
Papermaking   48
Printing and Bookmaking   50
The Clock   52
Black Powder and the Chemical Revolution   54

The Magnetic Compass 56

The Microscope 58

The Telescope 60

The Steam Engine 62

chapter four

THE AGE OF ELECTRICITY AND COMMUNICATION: (1799-1887) 64

The Battery 66

Anesthesia 68

Photography 70

The Electric Motor 72

The Telegraph 74

Chemical Fertilizers 76

The Internal Combustion Engine 78

Antiseptics 80

Plastics 82

The Phonograph 84

The Incandescent Bulb 86

chapter five

THE AGE OF THE ATOM: (1887-PRESENT) 88

Radio Broadcasting 90

The X ray 92

The Airplane 94

The Rocket 96

Antibiotics 98

The Nuclear Reactor 100

The Computer 102

Transistors and IC Chips 104

The Laser 106

Looking Ahead 108

Bibliography, Web Sites, and Invention Contests 109

Index 111

INTRODUCTION

IF YOU STOP AND THINK ABOUT IT, it seems pretty amazing that humans have come to dominate the world. Let's face it—stripped down to our birthday suits, we're really not much of a threat to the rest of the animal kingdom. Deer are faster, oxen are stronger, and lions have sharper teeth. Humans do have one major advantage, however, and that's our superior brains. Using our intelligence and imagination, we can solve problems and invent devices that not only protect us, but make our lives easier.

While it is true that some animals, including chimps and birds, use simple tools such as sticks to help them get food, we humans actually go out of our way to seek new and better ways of doing things. In addition to being inventive, we have the advantage of being able to communicate our thoughts to other people. This means that if someone thinks up a cool idea, he or she can tell someone else, and soon everybody is living in a whole new-and-improved way!

Over the course of human history, people have come up with millions of inventions that have helped them to live easier lives. While things like the shoehorn haven't had a major impact on our world, some, like the wheel, the radio, and the lightbulb, have literally changed the course of human history. In this book we're going to take a look at a number of important inventions that really shook up society. Every invention included here has in some way made a major change in the way people lived at the time it was developed. By reading through these pages, we hope that you'll discover just how much change technology has brought to our world, and maybe we'll inspire you to create some inventions of your own!

chapter one

THE

ANCIENT

WORLD

BEFORE 3500 B.C.

I N T H I S C H A P T E R , we're going to take a look at some of the important inventions of early humans—things developed before people kept records. To find out about life at those times we rely on evidence literally dug up by archaeologists who piece together the past. Naturally, some of the dates and times are a little sketchy, and as more evidence becomes available, the story of prehistory will continue to be revised.

In the Old Stone Age, 13,000 B.C. (a time that scientists call the Paleolithic period), there were no such things as patent searches or trademarks. Many inventions were made over and over again by different people working in different places at different times. Because these Stone Age technicians had to work with raw materials that nature provided, most of the early inventions were made of stone, bone, wood, and plant materials.

Unlike today, people in ancient times lived in isolated groups that only occasionally had contact with one another. Because of this, new ideas passed slowly from one area to another. Even so, by around 8000 B.C., at the start of the New Stone Age (a time scientists call the Neolithic period), most early inventions had spread throughout the known world.

THE HAND AX

Based on archaeological evidence from Africa, the first inventions appear to have been made more than two million years ago by creatures called *Homo habilis*, or "handy man," because of the devices they constructed. Back then, life was tough. People had to collect, scavenge, and hunt for food for a good part of the day. They ate seeds, fruit, roots, and even the leftover carcasses of animals killed by other predators. While human hands are quite good at gripping and manipulating things, they are limited when it comes to crushing, ripping, and opening hard objects. To get around this problem, humans first developed simple pebble tools, which eventually led to the hand ax.

Looking more like a fist-sized rock with a sharp edge than a well-honed modern tool, the hand ax was the first in a long line of "food processors" used for cutting and chopping everything from roots to leftover water buffalo.

HOW IT WORKS   The hand ax is actually a form of machine that scientists call a *wedge*. In its simplest form, a wedge is any wide, flat object that tapers to a thin edge. Wedges with a sharp edge are useful as cutting tools, and blunt wedges can be used to split things apart.

The first tools were probably stones that had naturally split to leave a sharp edge, which some enterprising early human decided to put to use. After a great deal of trial and error, humans discovered that they could make their own tools by taking two rocks and whacking them together at just the right angle.

While these first crude pebble tools were helpful, true hand axes made their appearance about one and a half million years later. By then, humans had discovered that certain types of rock, like flint and obsidian, would break with a conchoidal (shell-like) fracture, producing an extremely sharp edge. Instead of banging two rocks together with a great deal of force, they would take a hard round stone and gently strike it at an angle along the edge of the second stone, called the *core*. By breaking off many small pieces, they could eventually construct a sharp cutting tool from the core that would stand up to repeated use. Later still, humans discovered *pressure-flaking*, a technique where a pointed stick or bone was pressed against the edge of a flint core and even smaller flakes could be removed. With this new technique, humans were able to produce much more refined tools in a variety of shapes and sizes.

IMPACT   The use of hand axes and similar tools greatly changed the way early humans lived by reducing the time and effort needed to get food. In addition, sharp-edged cutting tools allowed humans to change their diet of mostly plants to one that included a great deal of high-protein meat. Some scientists believe the improved diet helped speed human evolution.

About 400,000 years ago, our ancestors had gotten so good at sharpening stones into different shapes that hand axes gave rise to other wedge-shaped tools like scrapers and knives. Soon, tools became weapons that could be used to defend against other predators, and slowly but surely, humans turned from being simply scavengers to being outright hunters.

CHILDREN OF THIS INVENTION   From its humble beginnings, the simple stone hand ax gave rise to a host of useful inventions, including spear and arrow points, and sickles for harvesting grains. Wedges form the backbone of many modern tools, too, including screwdrivers, chisels, and even pizza cutters!

Knife

Knife

Hand Ax

Scraper

In addition to stone axes, the prehistoric tool kit included scrapers and knife blades.

THE SPEAR

As with the hand ax, the spear was invented at a time when early humans were trying to eke out a living by collecting food. Over time, these individuals discovered that many tasty morsels were actually found underground. But it was hard to get the food out of the soil with their bare hands. Using pointed sticks to dig up food made the job easier—but the sticks often broke or became dull. They soon learned that burning the end of the stick in a fire not only made it easier to sharpen, but also hardened the point.

In all likelihood, spears came about because people discovered that pointy digging sticks could come in handy if they were attacked by a bear or an angry water buffalo. At first, humans used the spear purely as a defensive weapon, but it wasn't long before they realized that spears would make dandy tools for hunting. By hiding undercover, a group of hunters could ambush a large, slow-moving animal and use the spears to stab it until it was dead.

HOW IT WORKS   Even though they were hardened by fire, simple wooden spears would not stay sharp for very long. To make an effective spear, people needed a way to keep the end as sharp as their stone knives. Archaeological evidence from France suggests that by 45,000 years ago, hunters had learned that by making the point from rock and attaching it to a wooden shaft, they could have a solid spear with a point that could stand the test of time. In order to attach the stone point

A simple wooden spear was a multipurpose tool used for hunting and fishing and also for digging and moving large rocks.

to the spear, the wooden shaft was split at one end and the base of the point inserted. The end of the spear was then lashed tight with either vines or animal sinew to keep the point from falling out. As spears developed, hunters found that by tapering the back of the point, they could slip it farther into the shaft, making the whole weapon more secure.

IMPACT   With their spears in hand, humans really began to move up the economic ladder! No longer were they dependent on other animals to make a kill; they could hunt big game for themselves anytime they needed. What's more, by bringing down larger game, a group of hunters would have meat for several families for several days, which again freed up more time for other activities, like artwork. Finally, by working as a team, hunting parties and bands began to depend on one another more, which contributed to the development of simple societies.

CHILDREN OF THIS INVENTION   Indirectly, spears and spear-throwers showed early humans the power of the lever. Simple digging sticks were soon modified with stone heads, and specialized tools were developed. Archaeological evidence from Europe, Asia, and Africa suggests that as early as 250,000 years ago, people began using vines and sinews to attach handles to their stone hand axes. By using a short stick as a handle, they could get much more power when they chopped things. This gave rise to simple hammers, hatchets, and eventually the ax.

About 15,000 B.C. hunters developed the spear-thrower, long hooked sticks that allowed them to propel spears with much more force than simply throwing them by hand. Using these devices, hunters could go after big game.

ART

If you check out different lists of earthshaking inventions, for some reason, artworks of various types are often left off. While paintings and sculptures may be pleasant to look at, some people feel that they really don't have a practical value. According to some anthropologists, however, the rise of these art forms was the first step in the development of other important inventions such as writing, pottery, and even architecture. Through art, people explored size and shape and, for the first time, left an intentional record of how they saw the world around them. Like the use of stone tools and spears, artwork was invented many times by different people all over the world.

One of the most famous examples of ancient artwork can be found on the walls of caves of Altimira and Lascaux in what is now France. These detailed drawings from about 15,000 years ago clearly show scenes of people hunting, preparing food, and going about their other daily activities.

HOW IT WORKS Archaeological records show that as early as 100,000 years ago, people were decorating their spears and other tools with simple designs carved with stone knives. Some of these designs showed animals that were hunted, perhaps suggesting that these early hunter/artists felt a spiritual connection to their prey. By 30,000 years ago, small figurines carved out of bone, stone, and ivory had become widespread. Some of the most common kinds of these minisculptures were "Venus figures" showing what appear to be women dressed in simple clothes.

Artifacts reveal that about 20,000 years ago, people were not only carving sculptures of rock and bone but also molding them from clay. In the beginning, the

clay was simply dried in the sun, but later it was discovered that the clay could be made harder and stronger by placing it in a fire. This firing of clay, first used in art, was a critical step in making pottery.

In addition to sculpting, people also found they could record images by drawing and painting them on the surfaces of rocks. These paintings clearly showed that people had begun to experiment with different chemicals. By mixing water with ground-up minerals like iron and manganese oxide, humans were able to make different-colored paints that we can still recognize today.

IMPACT   From an archaeological standpoint, the development of art was critical because it provided scientists with the first real picture of how ancient humans lived. From cave drawings and other *pictographs*, early forms of writing began to develop, which opened the way for broader communication among different groups of people. The techniques used in making clay-fired sculptures were quickly adapted to making pottery and construction materials, which helped pave the way for villages and other large-scale settlements.

CHILDREN OF THIS INVENTION   Many anthropologists have linked these early forms of artwork to the spiritual development of humans. As early art forms developed, humans began to take great interest in the care of their dead. Careful ritual burials became common, and with them came religion.

Ancient humans began their art by carving figures in stone and ivory. These figures are believed to be simple "good luck" or fertility charms.

FARMING

As with artwork, farming isn't always considered to be an invention as much as a way of life. Before the invention of farming, however, people supported themselves by hunting, gathering, and scavenging for food. This meant that they were pretty much always on the move, either following the herds of game or looking for new places to forage.

Around 12,000 years ago, the last of the great ice ages was coming to an end, and the earth was going through some major climatic changes. Areas that had been desert began to get wet, and many of the large Ice Age mammals that depended on the shrinking grasslands of the tundra were facing extinction.

At the same time, human populations in these areas were beginning to grow, and people found it difficult to support themselves just by hunting and gathering.

HOW IT WORKS For people living in the Middle East, the main food source was wild grain like wheat, barley, or oats. Using sickles made of bone with sharp pieces of flint stuck into them, they would harvest the grain and take it back to

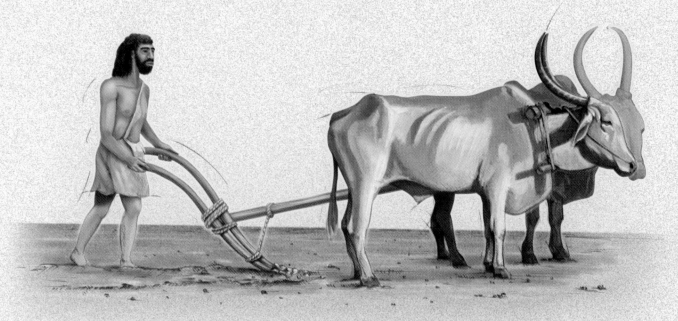

Digging sticks were very inefficient for turning over a large amount of earth. By about 3500 B.C., simple plows, which were made from wood and pushed by hand, were in use all over the Middle East.

their camp for grinding. Some of the seeds would get scattered on the ground and begin to grow where they fell. It wasn't long before people realized that they could simply spread seeds on the ground and grow the plants where they wanted to.

Most scientists believe that the first place widespread farming developed was in the Fertile Crescent, an area of the world that is now occupied by Iran and Iraq. In this region, wild wheat and barley were harvested and planted as early as 10,000 B.C.

Archaeological records show that 8,000 to 10,000 years ago, people also began to domesticate animals. The first domestic animals used for food were probably wild dogs and pigs because both of these animals are primarily scavengers, eating the leftovers from what other animals kill. Humans had plenty of leftovers, so they could provide these animals with ample food and get rid of their garbage at the same time!

Dogs and pigs are also relatively small and easy to catch. Later, people found that they could also keep larger animals like goats, sheep, and even cattle. Dogs were eventually trained to help control the herds of these other animals, so many people soon took them off the menu and placed them in the category of "man's best friend."

IMPACT Because crops took time to grow, people needed to stay near their farms, so they built semipermanent settlements. Often, they chose a place near a river or lake, because they had discovered that they could use extra water on the fields to grow bigger and better crops. As irrigation systems developed and farms became more productive, the first cities were born.

CHILDREN OF THIS INVENTION Since farmers could now grow far more food than they would need for themselves, they began to trade their surplus with people who specialized in crafts. Along with the concept of division of labor, the marketplace was born!

CITIES

Early humans had little use for permanent buildings. Living in the tropics, where it was warm year-round, and surviving as hunters and gatherers, they were constantly on the move in search of food. As hominids pushed into northern climates, their shelters were often made from natural caves that they could adapt for their own purposes. By about 400,000 years ago, people had learned enough basic building techniques to make temporary structures from grass, wood, and animal skins. Traces of huts from Terra Amata in southern France show that bent branches were often the building material of choice for these early dwellings.

With the beginning of agriculture and the need to "stay on the farm," the first true permanent structures were developed. In a sense, one of the first things to grow out of the agricultural revolution was the city!

HOW IT WORKS In order to take advantage of water for irrigation and fishing resources, most of the early cities were located near a large lake, a river, or the sea. While some of these early settlements still had huts made from grass, a growing trend was to build them out of stone.

Unfortunately, in many of the river valley regions, there wasn't always enough rock to build suitable structures. Drawing on their experience with making figures from clay, people turned to mud brick as the building material of choice. They discovered that it's much easier to stack bricks if they're all about the same size and shape, so before the ancient engineers made the bricks, they first built a wooden frame that served as a mold. The next step would be to take some soil, mix it with water until it was like a thick soup, and pour it into the mold. The mold was then placed in the sun for a few hours until the brick turned hard. Finally, the brick was taken out of the mold and stacked to cure for a few days before it was used in a structure.

Mud bricks worked well for areas where there was low rainfall, but in wet regions, they would wear away fairly quickly. Drawing on a technology that was first used in art, people found that by making the bricks out of pure clay, and then placing them in a fire, they would get a much harder brick that could stand up to many years of rain. By 4000 B.C., most structures in the Middle East that weren't made from stone were made from fired brick.

IMPACT   Once permanent cities were established, people started to "settle in." They needed rules to help control things like water rights and use of farmland. This led to the formation of the first governments. Cities also became centers of trade, where people from outlying lands could come to exchange goods. Of course, as different cities grew, so did the rivalries among them. Competition led to conflict and, ultimately, to warfare.

CHILDREN OF THIS INVENTION   To hold the bricks and stones together, people used a mortar made from *gypsum*, a mineral that dissolves in water and hardens when it dries. The common name for this material is plaster of Paris, and it's still being used today for walls and ceilings. As structures got bigger, people began to specialize in their design and construction, which in turn helped to spur the growth of the sciences of mathematics and architecture.

CLOTHING

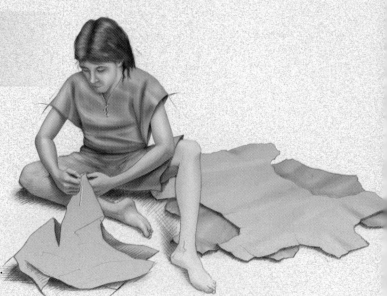

Early humans living in the tropical regions of Africa had little need to cover their bodies. Temperatures were warm, and abundant body hair provided a wonderful natural covering. As you might suspect because of their cooler climates, the first archaeological evidence of clothing came from China, Europe, and the mountainous areas of the Middle East. The first clothes weren't made from cloth, but were simply skins "borrowed" from other animals who had been lunch the week before!

To make leather wearable, skins were first soaked in water (sometimes boiled), usually with tree bark, which released a substance called *tannic acid*. This chemical made the skin softer and also helped to seal and preserve the material. Before "tanning," the skin was scraped clean of all its hair and fat. After several days of soaking, the leather was soft enough to wear.

HOW IT WORKS   Anyone who has ever felt natural horsehide or taken a nap on a genuine bearskin rug can tell you that in most cases, natural animal skins don't make comfortable clothing. Not only are they stiff and very rough, but unless they're treated properly, they smell really bad! As a result, most skins were used for shelter, and processed leather became the clothing of choice. Archaeological evidence from France shows that individual pieces of leather were sewn together with leather strips using bone needles as early as 20,000 years ago.

Archaeologists believe that the first true textiles, or woven fabrics, developed around 12,000 years ago, at the same time many of the other fine arts were developing. Although cloth fabric was a new idea, evidence from the Middle East shows that people had been weaving for some time. They probably learned the art of weaving by watching birds build nests, and they quickly adapted the process for making baskets, mats, and shelters.

In the beginning, natural fibers taken from wild grasses were used as the material, but as farming developed, people discovered that cultivated fibers were consistently stronger and easier to work with. By 3000 B.C., flax and hemp were being cultivated to make thread, and cotton was used in India around 2000 B.C.

IMPACT   In addition to being used for clothing, fabrics were important for trade. Long before there was money, people used cloth as a type of currency, trading it for food and other goods. The desire for special types of cloth encouraged people to travel great distances, which paved the way for the creation of established trade routes. Finally, as cities grew, more and more people took on specialized tasks. No longer were people "jacks-of-all-trades." Instead, they became farmers, weavers, or potters. Division of labor had become a reality.

CHILDREN OF THIS INVENTION   Besides clothing, the art of textile making was used for other practical purposes. Mats, tapestries, thatched roofs for houses, and even reed boats were developed from this same basic skill.

Before any fiber can be used to make fabric, it must first be processed. Flax and hemp, which produce a very coarse, rough fiber, were first soaked in water and then beaten with rocks to get the softer inner material out. Since the fibers produced by individual plants were too short to be of any use by themselves, people had to twist them together to make thread. This process, known as spinning, became common around 4,000 years ago, and it's still used, although today large machines make the thread.

POTTERY

The earliest forms of pottery look like baskets because they were made the same way. Borrowing a technique that was first used in making thread, people would take clay and roll it between their hands until it made long ribbons. These clay threads were then coiled on top of one another until they formed a vessel.

One of the most important inventions to grow out of the agricultural revolution was pottery. As hunters, people pretty much lived day to day on whatever they could catch or find. There was little extra food, so there was really no reason to have anything other than baskets or leather pouches to store it in. Once people started growing their own food, the situation changed rapidly.

Because many crops ripen together, farmers often have a huge amount of food available at one time, and none the rest of the year. The trick is to try and make the harvest last as long as possible by storing excess grain in some type of container. At first, baskets and bags were probably used to do this, but where you have seeds, you almost always have mice, whose sharp teeth would make short work of a woven basket. Not wanting to see their hard work go to waste, people needed to come up with storage containers that animals couldn't get into.

Archaeological evidence shows that in some cases, people had attempted to carve containers from natural stone. However, this was very time-consuming and an almost impossible task using simple stone tools. Borrowing a technique that was first used in sculpture, then buildings, they began to make "synthetic stone" pots of clay and mud. In the Middle East, the first evidence of clay pottery goes back to about 7000 B.C., in the area that is now Iran. Recent discoveries in Japan suggest that pottery was first used there as early as 12,700 years ago.

In the case of Japanese pottery, it wasn't agriculture that was the driving force, but fishing. In addition to using their pots to store seafood, people found that they could also use them for cooking things like sea vegetables and shellfish.

HOW IT WORKS   As with the first mud bricks, these simple clay pots were placed in the sun to dry. To speed up the drying, people discovered that you could dig a pit and place the pots inside with a fire. The hotter the fire, the harder the clay would become. As time went on, fire pits were replaced by stone and brick ovens specially designed to bake pottery. People discovered that by using hollow reeds to blow air into the fire, they could get temperatures really hot, and by about 4000 B.C. the kiln was born!

IMPACT   By using clay jars and pots to store food and water, people could now make their supplies last through winter months and times of famine. Pottery also made the trade in surplus goods more efficient, and, as we'll see in the next chapter, made the need for some type of money essential.

CHILDREN OF THIS INVENTION   As the fires used for making pottery got hotter and the fuels changed from wood to charcoal, the first glass started to appear. Glass forms when sand-sized particles of certain minerals are heated hot enough that they actually melt and fuse together. The first manufactured glass was probably the result of some sand accidentally getting fired in a very hot kiln along with some clay pots. People soon learned that by mixing together silica sand and soda ash, they could make glass anytime they wanted!

Stone kilns were used to bake pottery to make it hard. Before firing, a special mixture of materials was used to coat the clay, which "glazed" the pots. This not only preserved the pots but also helped make them watertight.

RAFTS, DUGOUTS, AND BOATS

It's hard to know exactly when humans first took to the water, but it's a safe bet that long before they used carts, people were using the waterways as a quick and easy mode of transportation. Before true boats were developed, people probably made simple rafts of logs, branches, reeds, or other naturally floating material. Building on their skills of basket weaving, people found that it was easy to lash together enough material to support the weight of several individuals. In fact, some anthropologists think that people may have used this type of raft to sail across fairly large stretches of ocean as early as 20,000 years ago. This would help to explain the spread of peoples throughout Polynesia and Australia.

WHO As people settled along rivers and lakes, and farming and fishing began to replace hunting and gathering as a way of life, humans began to develop the first true boats. The earliest surviving boat comes from Holland, and it's simply a thick log about 13 feet (4 meters) long, hollowed out to form a dugout canoe. Known as the Pesse boat because of the town that it was found in, it's more than 8,400 years old. It's hard to tell just how long people were using this technique before the Pesse boat was built because the wood from which these vessels were made normally rots away over time. In Yorkshire, England,

Dugout canoes are quite easy to build. You start by chipping away some material on the top side to flatten it out. Then, by using a series of small fires on the top, you can burn and chip away enough material with a stone ax to fit a full-grown person inside.

scientists have found a wooden paddle preserved in a peat bog that dates back to 7500 B.C., so in all likelihood, this technology is at least 10,000 years old.

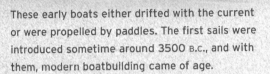

These early boats either drifted with the current or were propelled by paddles. The first sails were introduced sometime around 3500 B.C., and with them, modern boatbuilding came of age.

HOW IT WORKS In the Middle East, where timber was scarce, people had to turn to other material for building their boats. Along the Tigris and Euphrates rivers, a light wooden framework much like a basket was built of branches. Hides and skins were then sewn over the top of the frame to make a small vessel big enough for one or two people. These *quffas* have been used for more than 3,000 years and are still in use in the Middle East today. Similar boats have also been found in Europe and around England and Ireland.

The heyday of early boatbuilding took place in Egypt. Along the Nile River, timber for boatbuilding is scarce, but papyrus reeds are very abundant and float well when they are cut and dried. As early as 5000 B.C., people were building rafts from bundles of papyrus reeds lashed together. Later, the rafts were designed with sides to prevent people and cargo from falling over the edge, and they were given a pointed front to help cut through the water.

IMPACT As vessels became more seaworthy, people began to explore new areas in search of treasures and resources. With boats, people established regular trade routes, which not only allowed them to trade goods, but also to exchange ideas and share technology around the world!

CHILDREN OF THIS INVENTION Over time, people realized that wind could not only push boats, but also be put to use on land as well. While the first windmills were still several centuries in the future, their basic design came from that of a sail, which was first used on Egyptian reed boats.

THE AXLE

In most books about inventions, the wheel, and not the axle, is listed as one of the most important things ever developed, but without an axle to turn on, a wheel is useless. Don't believe me? Just try rolling something on top of a wheel. It won't work!

Long before someone got the bright idea of putting wheels on carts, people had been using them to make pottery. Turntables, which were really flat wheels turned sideways, had been used for several hundred years to help shape and smooth clay. Nobody knows who first came up with the idea for a wheel, but they've been used for a very long time. Most historians believe that the first wheels used for transportation date back to around 3500 B.C. when they were placed on simple carts.

Drawings on pottery and actual pieces of wheels found by archaeologists suggest that the Middle East was the birthplace of the modern wheel, although examples of early wheels have also been found in Europe and Asia. In all likelihood, no one person invented the wheel, but it was probably developed in many different locations by many different individuals trying to get a break from dragging things around.

HOW IT WORKS The first step in the invention of the wheel was the roller. Rollers can be made by placing some smooth tree trunks underneath large, flat objects. The

The first vehicle to make use of the wheel was not a cart or a chariot, but simply a one-wheel device similar to the modern wheelbarrow.

problem with rollers is that to make them work, you have to keep picking them up and moving them in front of the object you're trying to move. This takes a lot of time and effort. Also, if your timing is off just a little bit, the object you're moving will slide off the rollers and come crashing to a halt. Now you can see why it's the axle and not the wheel that is so important! By placing an axle between two supports and sticking a wheel in the middle, people had a device that could roll without the hassle of the roller.

While potters' wheels and millstones were made of stone, few if any transport wheels were made this way. They would have been too heavy, and it would have taken too much effort to make them. While it may seem like the logical approach, wooden wheels were not made by cutting off cross sections of tree trunks. This was probably tried, but because of the way it grows, wood is very weak when cut in cross sections. Any heavy load placed on a wheel made this way would cause the wheel to quickly split and crack.

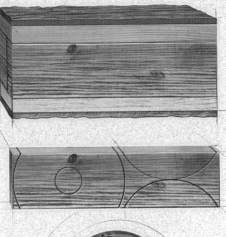

Most wooden wheels were not made by cutting across a tree trunk, but instead were made from three pieces of wood connected together. In this way, the grain of each piece of wood would be running in the same direction, making the wheel quite strong.

IMPACT   Like the boat, wheels and axles made it possible for people to transport heavy loads over great distances. Unlike a boat, wheeled vehicles could travel over dry land, and soon roads began to replace waterways as the major trade routes. This also meant that people didn't have to settle near large bodies of water. As a result, villages and cities could now be built inland, where other resources were abundant.

CHILDREN OF THIS INVENTION   Just think how many things have wheels on and in them: cars, bikes, trains, skateboards, scooters, grandfather clocks, doorknobs, even the faucets on your sink. The list is endless and it's all because of the invention of the axle!

chapter two

THE

METAL

AGE

AS WE SAW IN THE LAST CHAPTER, by about 3500 B.C. many changes had taken place in the ways people lived and how they organized their societies. While many people still supported themselves by hunting and gathering food, many others had taken up farming as a way of making a living. As more people settled into cities, one of the major changes was the division of labor. Instead of each person having to get food, make pottery, and do all the other tasks necessary for life, people could now begin to specialize in different jobs.

People were exchanging goods among themselves, and different cities were linked together by well-defined trade routes sometimes stretching hundreds of miles. As the Neolithic period drew to a close, people found that they needed other ways besides talking to communicate their ideas. Soon, the first written words and maps began to appear. To help with trade, money and systems of measurement were also developed. Finally, for the first time, metals instead of stone were used for tools and weapons.

WRITING

The need for writing was another outgrowth of the agricultural revolution. By 3500 B.C., people living in the early cities along the Tigris, Euphrates, and Nile rivers were not only farming, but they were also beginning to divide up the land. As they became more specialized in their work and trading goods became a way of life, it became harder and harder to know who owned what. Some sort of permanent record-keeping method was needed.

By about 3000 B.C., cuneiform-style writing began to spread to other people throughout the Middle East. Clay tablets have been found with modified cuneiform writing of the Babylonian, Assyrian, and Hittite languages as well as Sumerian.

As with most of the early inventions, it's hard to place exactly when the first written words were developed. While there is good evidence that some form of writing was used in China as early as 4000 B.C., archaeologists have yet to find any direct evidence that has been preserved. The first preserved examples of writing come from a group of Middle Eastern people known as Sumerians, in about 3200 B.C.

HOW IT WORKS   As we saw in the last chapter, the origins of modern writing can be traced to the time of ancient artists, who used pictures to describe things and events that were important to them. The key to writing involved taking complex pictures and turning them into a set of standard symbols that had very specific meanings.

Using clay tablets and a sharp stick called a stylus, the Sumerian people living in Mesopotamia developed the first form of true writing called *cuneiform*. The original cuneiform writing did not have an alphabet. Instead, there were more than 1,200 different symbols to represent things like names, numbers, and objects.

At about the same time, *hieroglyphics*, another symbolic writing form, appeared in Egypt. In hieroglyphic writing, the symbols are more like pictures than simple wedge forms, but they are much more standardized than the drawings done in earlier times.

As writing spread, it became very difficult to keep track of such a large number of different symbols. To make life easier, a new concept developed. Instead of having symbols represent objects, people started to use specific symbols to represent sounds used in the spoken language. By doing this, it was possible to put together a few different sound symbols in a group to represent a spoken word. These "phonographic" symbols were the beginnings of the modern forms of language used in most of the world today.

IMPACT   Written language not only allowed people to record important information such as who owned what piece of land, but it also allowed individuals to preserve this information. For the first time, rules of how to live were spelled out, and the first laws were developed. In addition, people could now begin to record important events in their history. From an archaeological standpoint, once writing began, much of the guesswork came to an end.

CHILDREN OF THIS INVENTION   The final chapter in the development of modern writing happened around 2000 B.C. and is called the alphabetic principle. The first true alphabet was developed by Semitic-speaking people (probably Phoenicians) in the Middle East. This written language was then adopted and modified by the people of ancient Greece. Modern variations of this ancient form of script can be seen in Hebrew and Arabic texts, and in fact the word alphabet comes from the first two letters in the Hebrew language, *aleph* and *beth*.

Within the halls of the pyramids and other structures of ancient Egypt, long rows of hieroglyphic symbols have been found.

MATHEMATICS

The idea of mathematics as a critical invention may sound funny, but math, like writing, became very important for record keeping once people began to trade with one another. In ancient times, hunters and farmers had no need for math. They would simply take what they needed from the land without ever wondering how much they had. As cities grew and people began to specialize in different tasks, things got more complicated. A farmer who needed some storage jars needed to know how much grain he had to trade with the potter in exchange for his goods.

As with writing, number systems seemed to get their start in Mesopotamia around 3000 B.C., with examples of different number systems having been found on Sumerian, Babylonian, and Akkadian tablets. People in Babylonia developed a very complex number system based on 60 different digits. Later, in Egypt, people developed a simpler system based on the number 10. Ten is a natural number system for humans because most of us have 10 fingers and 10 toes.

HOW IT WORKS   Math really starts with counting, and undoubtedly, early people used their fingers and toes to count just as young children do now, but counting alone is not math. Like writing, true mathematics began when people started using symbols to represent certain numbers of things.

In those ancient times, people already had the idea of using a place-value system to represent large numbers. An example of place value is what we use today in our own system: ones column, tens column, hundreds column, and so on.

While the decimal system in Egypt had symbols totally different from what we use today, papyrus scrolls from 1900 B.C. and 1700 B.C. showed that early Egyptians were already well acquainted not only with addition, but also subtraction, multiplication, and division.

IMPACT   With the development of mathematics, people not only had a way of keeping track of trades and personal property, but they were able to begin to measure the world around them. This led to new construction techniques and the first maps.

CHILDREN OF THIS INVENTION The number system most often used in the world today has Arabic numerals, and as the name suggests, it was probably developed in the Middle East, although historians are not certain. There is growing evidence that the system was first used in what is now India about 2,500 years ago. The number zero was a Hindu invention, beginning as a small dot to represent a vacant space. The Maya of Central America also developed the concept of zero independently of Western culture for their mathematical operations.

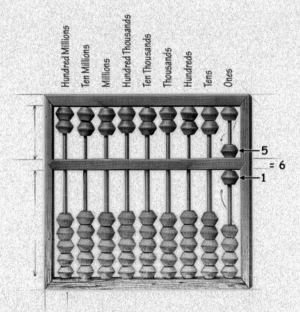

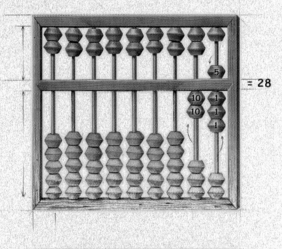

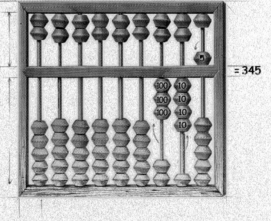

Today, we have pocket calculators to help us do math, but in the early days people used an ingenious device called an *abacus*. First developed around 2000 b.c. in Babylonia, the original design was nothing more than a sand-covered board on which little clay counting beads were moved. A modern abacus has a wooden frame with a bar going across the middle. Wooden beads are suspended by wires with two beads above the bar and five below the bar on each wire. Each wire represents one decimal place with the one on the right being the "ones" column, the second one being the "tens" column and so on. Each bead below the bar represents one unit for the column and each bead above the bar represents five units for the column. Beads are counted by putting them against the bar.

MEASUREMENT

easurement and math go hand in hand. Mathematics helps you count and keep track of how many things you have, but measurement allows you to compare things fair and square. Let's say that you're a farmer in ancient Babylonia, and you want to trade your grain for a really neat pair of shoes. The shoemaker says the price is five baskets of grain but he doesn't say how big the baskets should be. You give him five really small baskets, which would be far less grain than one really *big* basket! In this case, the number five is not important, it's the size of the basket that counts. Once people started trading goods and owning property, there had to be some way of quantifying how much "stuff" they had.

While systems of measurements developed all over the world, the first records come from both Babylonia and Egypt around 3000 B.C.

HOW IT WORKS   For measurements to be practical, you have to have a standard that everybody agrees on, which never changes, and to which other things can be compared. Standards can be arbitrary, which means they can be completely made up, or they can be designed around some natural quantity.

For a standard to be useful, it has to be something that is common and easy for most people to get ahold of. For this reason, most of the early standards were based on human body parts.

The rulers of ancient Egypt realized that the size of a person's arm could vary,

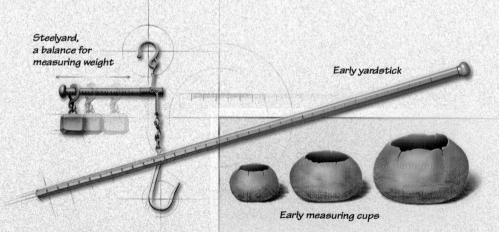

Steelyard,
a balance for
measuring weight

Early yardstick

Early measuring cups

There are two basic types of measurement: mass, or weight, which measures how heavy something is; and length, which measures how long something is. Volume, which measures the capacity of a container for things like liquid or grain, is really length measurements in three dimensions.

so they set up a *royal master cubit*, which was carved on a chunk of black granite so that other cubit sticks could be measured against it and periodically checked. The official length of the royal master cubit is now known to be 524 millimeters (about 21 inches) and it was further divided into 28 digits. As you might have guessed, a "digit" was the approximate width of the finger of a grown man. Four digits equaled one "palm" and five digits was a "hand." For some reason, Egyptians didn't care much for feet. The foot (12 inches) that is commonly used today was developed by the ancient Babylonians.

IMPACT   Once people had a way of standardizing measurement, they could fairly compare the amount of goods they had. The concept of wealth came into play, and often, to accumulate more wealth, people went to war. Measurement, like math, was also crucial in the development of architecture and maps. For the first time, people began to get an idea of just how large their world was.

CHILDREN OF THIS INVENTION   The development of weights and measures led to the invention of the first true money. The *shekel* and *talent*, which are often mentioned in the Bible, were originally standards for weight, but soon they became units of money. According to one ancient conversion table, one sacred mina was equal to 60 shekels, and the sacred talent was equal to 3,000 shekels.

One of the first standard measurements for length was the cubit, which appears to be of Egyptian origin. A cubit was defined by the length of the human arm from the tip of the extended fingers to the bottom of the elbow. As you might expect, depending on the size of a person, the length of a cubit could vary quite a bit.

1 cubit

MONEY

Today, it's hard to imagine a world without money. It's such an important part of our modern-day world that most people forget that it's an invention. Just like writing and math, money developed as a result of widespread trade and ownership of property. Before money, traders depended on the barter system, which worked something like this: If I'm a potter and you're a fisherman, I can trade you a clay jug for a certain amount of fish and we go on our merry way. But let's say I want some deer steaks, and the hunter down the road already has enough pots but really wants some fish. Now I have to try and arrange a three-way trade with you to try and get the goods I need. As you can see, things could get quite complicated in a hurry!

The answer to these complex trading problems was for people to come up with a common material that everybody wanted, which could be swapped back and forth. It's from these early traders around 3000 B.C. in the Middle East and Egypt that our modern monetary system was born.

According to writings by the Greek philosopher Herodotus, the first crude coins were invented by the Lydian people of what is now western Turkey in the year 687 B.C. These coins were made from electrum, a naturally occurring combination of gold and silver.

HOW IT WORKS   Before coinage, the first forms of currency were either materials that were relatively rare, or things that everybody needed, such as cattle, sacks of grain, glass beads, cowrie shells, and, of course, precious metals. By trading for these items, people now had something they could collect and "cash in" for goods anytime they needed.

Because native metals were relatively rare and in high demand for use in jewelry and other ornaments, gold, silver, and copper quickly became the money

Early coins were punched with designs by the mint that issued them.

of choice among most traders. Using balance scales, traders would weigh small amounts of these metals and swap them for goods. This was somewhat time-consuming, so by 2500 B.C., Egyptian merchants began using standard-sized metal rings for trade. Later, around 2200 B.C., Cappadocian rulers issued the first "state" money in the form of silver bars or ingots.

Coins were very popular because they were easy to carry, they didn't wear out too fast, and they contained precious metals so they could always be melted down. One of the biggest problems with coins of the past was that people would shave them down to take away some of the metal. These lighter coins could then be passed off with the same value as the standard ones and the shaver could pocket some extra metal! This problem became so bad that by Greek and Roman times, coins started to have a raised ridge along their edges so that any "shaving" would be noticed right away.

IMPACT   As money systems became more developed, it became easier for people to trade back and forth, which greatly expanded commerce and industry around the world. By having money with a set value, people no longer had to store goods. Instead, they could save money, which could be spent at any time.

CHILDREN OF THIS INVENTION   Almost as soon as money came into common use, people began to get the idea that they could borrow and lend it. From these early transactions, today's modern banking industry developed, along with the stock market and, of course, taxes.

METALLURGY AND SMELTING

In the first chapter, we noted that in both the Paleolithic and Neolithic periods, humans were limited to using raw, unprocessed materials like wood, stone, and bone for tools. On occasion, people would also come across certain native metals like gold and silver, which are relatively soft and melt at fairly low temperatures. Well before 5000 B.C., people were working them into ornaments and jewelry by pounding them and heating them in campfires. These metals weren't really good for tools, however, because they were too soft. As cities grew and technology developed, people needed stronger, more durable tools and weapons. They turned to refined metals for the answer.

It seems that, like so many other useful inventions, the smelting and refining of metals came about in many places at about the same time. Dating from about 3200 B.C., Egyptian artifacts made of refined copper clearly show that the technology was in place there. Within a hundred years, the technology had spread throughout much of the Middle East.

HOW IT WORKS   In all probability the first processed metals came about by accident when some folks sitting around a roaring campfire dropped a piece of

In order to extract as much pure metal as possible from the ore, people used a blowpipe to add air and make a fire hotter.

copper ore into the fire. The next morning, they discovered a lump of almost pure copper sitting in the ashes. By heating it again, they found that they could get rid of even more impurities, and the art of smelting was born!

Over time, people discovered that in order to get a more controlled and hotter fire, they could use charcoal instead of wood as a fuel. Soon, campfires gave way to special furnaces, which were almost certainly adapted from the kilns used for making pottery.

While copper was the first metal to be used for tools, it was soft and bent easily. By mixing tin with copper, early metallurgists could make a bronze tool that could really stand the test of time.

The use of metals really took a big step forward around 3000 B.C. with another discovery. In the Taurus Mountains located in southern Turkey, copper ore is found mixed with the mineral cassiterite, which is one of the main ores of tin. Again, probably by accident, these two ores were smelted together and the result was the birth of the Bronze Age.

IMPACT Bronze is a metal that is called an alloy because it's really a mixture of tin and copper. It looks very much like copper, only it's much harder and can hold a very sharp edge, which makes it ideal for swords, knives, and other cutting instruments. With the production of copper and bronze, people now had tools, vessels, and weapons that could stand up to repeated use and also be made into almost any shape.

CHILDREN OF THIS INVENTION Over time, the same types of production techniques used for making copper and bronze were used on iron, which is a very abundant element. The big problem is that iron doesn't melt until it reaches about 2700°F (1500°C). As a result, iron had to be heated and hammered in order to get it into the proper shape. The first full-scale use of iron started in about 1400 B.C. with the Chalybes, a tribe living under the Hittite people in Mesopotamia. By about 1200 B.C., their methods of making iron spread to the Middle East, Europe, northern Africa, and even China.

IRRIGATION

Lack of water has always been a problem when it comes to growing enough food. As cities grew in China, Egypt, and the Middle East, more people depended on farming for food. People soon realized that they couldn't always rely on natural rainfall to provide enough water for their crops. Because of this, irrigation systems were developed to provide water, even when there was no rain.

As early as 4000 B.C., people living around the Nile River in Egypt and in the Tigris and Euphrates valleys in the Middle East discovered that they didn't need rain to water their crops. With a little engineering, they could use the rivers as a continuous source of water.

HOW IT WORKS   Farmers living in the river floodplains found that in the late summer, after the floodwaters had receded, they still had a hard time getting enough water to keep their crops growing. Undoubtedly, some tried to carry water from the rivers in clay jugs, but anyone who has ever tried to carry a bucketful of water even a short distance knows that this is hard work. There had to be a better way, and as it turned out, the answer was gravity.

By digging channels to the rivers upstream of the fields, people discovered that they could divert water from the river directly to the fields where they needed it. The problem was that many of these canals had to be miles (kilometers) long and took an entire community working together to dig and maintain. It's not surprising that as agriculture and the need for irrigation grew, organized governments and laws controlling the water also developed. In Egypt, by about 3000 B.C., records show that the land was already divided into water provinces (large rectangular sections cut by irrigation canals). Each province had its own governors called *adj mer*, which meant "digger of canals," and they were the ones who were responsible for making sure there was enough water for the fields.

IMPACT   With the use of irrigation, farmers could continuously grow enough food to support ever larger populations of people. As a result, cities expanded, often crossing into another group's territory. This led to conflicts over water rights, which sometimes resulted in war.

CHILDREN OF THIS INVENTION   In order to maintain controls over irrigation systems, laws governing their use were set down by local rulers. In Babylonia, the Code of Hammurabi spelled out in detail how these canals were to be cared for and called for stiff penalties for anyone who violated water-use rules. From these early codes came many of the other civil laws that we have today.

Probably the most well-known example of early irrigation techniques comes from Babylon around 1750 B.C. Here, the great ruler Hammurabi promoted the development of a system of brick-lined canals that were covered with natural asphalt mortar to keep them from leaking. During its peak time, this irrigation system criss-crossed more than 10,000 square miles (25,900 km²) (about the size of the state of Vermont) and supported over 15 million people.

WATERWHEELS

Having gained a great deal of experience in digging canals for irrigation, people soon discovered that the energy of flowing water could also be put to work. Since people first started using grains for food, one of the biggest problems had been grinding the grains into flour. At first they did it by hand, using large stone mortars and pestles. Later, they used a team of oxen fastened with yokes to a large grindstone as a source of power.

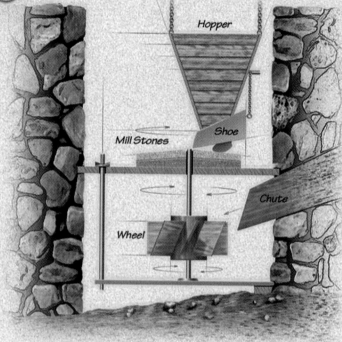

The first waterwheels had vertical shafts and were turned when fast-flowing streams hit the paddles on the bottom.

As with many of the early inventions, waterwheels were almost certainly invented in different locations at different times, but the first records of these clever devices come from about 3000 B.C. in the hilly parts of southwestern Asia, near what is now Turkey.

HOW IT WORKS   The idea of the waterwheel probably came from adapting a horizontal grindstone that was powered by oxen. By adding wooden paddles to the shaft on which a millstone was connected and placing it near a fast-moving stream, farmers could use water brought in through a channel to turn the stone. These vertical-shaft waterwheels were very popular in ancient Greece and northern Europe because they didn't require a great deal of engineering to build and use.

By about 100 B.C., the Greek type of vertical-shaft mill was turned on its side, making a horizontal-shaft wheel. The first of these, called an undershot wheel, works by water flowing underneath the wheel and pushing against a series of paddles. Undershot wheels were very inefficient, but they were easy to construct and could be set up in a natural stream channel.

IMPACT   Both undershot and overshot (see caption below) wheels were described in detail in the book *De architectura*, written by the Roman engineer Vitruvius about 27 B.C. These types of mills allowed large-scale industry to develop and were the principal source of power used throughout the world for about 2,000 years until the steam engine was invented.

CHILDREN OF THIS INVENTION   Even though horizontal-shaft wheels (undershot and overshot wheels) were much more efficient and produced more power than the Greek-style vertical-shaft wheel, they had one slight drawback: They turned in the wrong direction. How do you change vertical rotation to horizontal rotation? Easy—you invent gears! As with the wheel, no one knows for sure where the gear came from but it seems to have gotten its start somewhere around 100 B.C. and spread quickly throughout the Middle East and Europe. Gears not only solved the problem of direction, but by using different-sized gears connected together, people were able to change the speed of the device at will. If you want to see modern gears in action, just take a look at the back wheel of a mountain bike!

As the Greeks developed the undershot wheel, Roman engineers discovered that they could generate more power by using water falling over the wheel. Overshot wheels were more complex because not only did they have to build the wheel and set it in place, but they also had to construct a dam and sluiceway to carry the water down to hit the top of the wheel.

MAPS

By 1000 B.C., people were using boats, carts, and horses to travel and trade over greater and greater distances. In making their journeys, one of the biggest problems they faced was that they didn't always know where they were going and, once they got there, how to get back home. Unlike today, when you can have a satellite in space send a message to a computer in your car to tell you where you are, people in the past had to rely on landmarks, the words of strangers, and their wits. What the travelers of the world really needed was an accurate road map!

The first attempt at making a world map appears to have been made around 800 B.C. in Babylonia, with Babylonia in the center of the map and the rest of the world around it. Later, as Greek and Roman legions pushed the boundaries of the known world farther and farther, maps of what is now Africa, Europe, and western Asia were developed. It was just a matter of time before an accurate world map was produced.

HOW IT WORKS   While accurate world maps are relatively recent inventions, the first local maps may be as much as 12,000 years old. These simple drawings found carved on bones in what is now Russia seem to represent an area where people of the time lived or traveled, but they lacked two important details that modern maps have: scale and direction. Scale is important because it tells you how far a real distance is, when it is compared to the distance on the map. Without something to tell you direction, you won't know which way you're supposed to head!

One of the reasons it took so long to make reliable maps was because people didn't have a fixed point on which to base direction. On local maps, they used natural landmarks like mountains and rivers to set direction, but on a global scale, the features were too small. Around 600 B.C., in Miletus, which is now part of Turkey, a Greek philosopher named Anaximander found the key by looking up to the stars.

IMPACT   Once people had accurate maps with which to travel, they were free to venture farther and farther from home. With bigger boats to carry them and maps and stars to guide them, explorers could now lead the world into a whole new age of discovery.

CHILDREN OF THIS INVENTION   Using the stars as a reference, Anaximander started to make other measurements of the earth. It is reported that he was the first person to build an astrolabe, a device used for measuring angles between Earth, the Sun, and the stars. By using an astrolabe to measure how high Polaris (the North Star) is above the horizon (the point where the ground and sky meet), you can tell not only which way north is, but also how far north or south of the equator you are! The astrolabe and early maps led to the development of other astronomical instruments and the system of longitude and latitude that all navigators and cartographers use today.

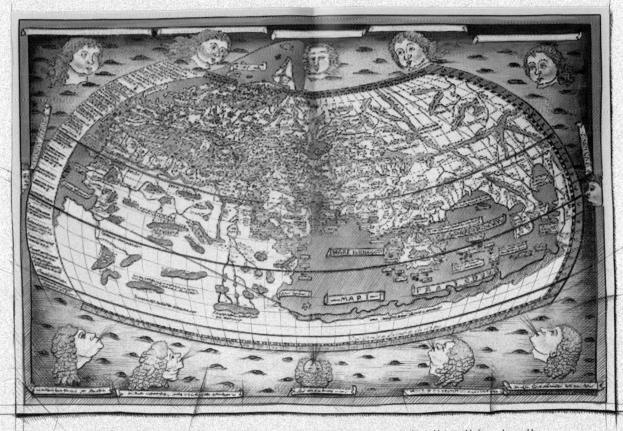

In A.D. 150, Claudius Ptolemaeus, a noted Greek astronomer and mathematician, drew the first full-scale world map, which became the standard for close to a thousand years.

chapter three

THE

AGE OF

DISCOVERY

A.D. 1 - 1799

As WE ENTER THE FIRST YEAR OF THE COMMON ERA, (as the time after B.C. is often called), we see that the world is primed for some major technological breakthroughs. Most of the larger cities and trading centers have been established for more than a thousand years, and in much of the world, agriculture has all but replaced hunting as a way of life.

The use of bronze and iron for tools has become commonplace, and people are experimenting with making new types of materials. With maps in hand, traders and explorers have begun to venture out into the open seas, daring to explore uncharted waters, and every major cultural group has its own form of writing, mathematics, and calendar. Still, these are only available to a few privileged individuals of high rank. The common folk have limited knowledge of these things, but the times are about to change.

Toward the end of the last century B.C., people began to experiment with chemicals, lenses, magnets, and other "curious" phenomena. These experiments would ultimately lead to the discovery of not only a microscopic world here on Earth, but a whole new universe in the distant heavens.

PAPERMAKING

One of the big problems with early forms of writing was that the cuneiform clay tablets used by the Babylonians took a tremendous amount of time to prepare and were difficult to carry. Around 3000 B.C., Egyptian scribes found that they could make a lighter writing material from papyrus reeds.

While papyrus scrolls were better than clay, they were still very time-consuming to produce. Like the Egyptians, early Chinese scribes had learned to make scrolls from either bamboo or silk.

HOW IT WORKS   According to the most popular Chinese legend, a gentleman by the name of Cai Lun first invented paper. Cai Lun was a member of the imperial court and was in charge of keeping official records. In a report to the emperor that he filed in A.D. 105, he said that he needed a new material to write on. He felt that bamboo was too heavy and silk was too expensive, so he began to look for an alternative.

Experimenting with different materials, he mixed together pieces of tree bark, fishnets (hemp fibers), and bamboo into a big pot with water, and used a mortarlike device

To make scrolls, the Egyptians cut the inside fibers of papyrus reeds into long strips and dried them in the sun. Then the strips were laid side by side on a flat, smooth surface, and a second set of strips was laid out across the first. The whole mass of strips was then soaked with water and pressed tightly together. The sap of the reeds acted like a glue to cement the two layers together. To finish the sheet off, it was hammered smooth and then allowed to dry in the sun. Individual sheets of papyrus were then glued together and rolled up on sticks to make a papyrus scroll 20 to 50 feet (6 to 15 m) long.

to pound the mixture into a thick pulp. He then rolled out this mushy material over a fine screen and let it dry. The result was a lightweight writing material that was both thin and durable, and the first true paper had been created.

IMPACT   Papermaking remained exclusively a Chinese art until A.D. 751, when Islamic armies captured several Chinese soldiers who knew the trade. These individuals were brought back to the city of Samarkand, where they trained others to make paper from mulberry and other types of bark. Within 200 years, papermaking had spread throughout the Middle East, eventually reaching Europe. With the spread of paper came the spread of knowledge because lightweight documents could now travel as easily as people.

CHILDREN OF THIS INVENTION   With the technology of papermaking firmly established, people had a cheap, durable material on which to write, draw, and decorate. This new material inspired people to experiment with mass producing written words, which opened the world to printing and bookmaking.

In ancient China, many different fibers were used to make paper including tree bark, rice, and bamboo. The plant material was first mashed up and placed in a tub of water to soak. A fine screen was used to lift even layers of fibers from the water. After draining, the wet sheets of fibers were lifted off the screen and placed on a wall to dry.

PRINTING AND BOOKMAKING

For letters and other documents that had only one use, writing by hand was easy enough, but for documents and designs that had to be reproduced over and over again, there were problems. Each copy took a tremendous amount of time, and there was a good chance that mistakes would happen. As a result, ancient Chinese artists began to look for ways to copy documents mechanically, and the concept of printing was developed.

HOW IT WORKS

Block printing made it possible to make hundreds of copies of the same document from a single master, but chiseling each page into the woodblock took a great deal of time, and if you made a mistake there was no way to correct it. You had to start cutting the entire block all over again! The next big printing innovation was movable type. In 1045, a Chinese printer by the name of Bi Sheng tried something new. Instead of cutting each block individually, he made a complete set of Chinese characters out of clay and fired them in a kiln to make them rock-hard. He then took the letters and set them upside down in an iron tray filled with hot wax.

When the wax cooled, it hardened, locking the letters into place. By rolling the ink over the letters and pressing a piece of paper against them, he was able to

The first attempts at printing in China go back to around A.D. 400. Artists discovered that they could take flat stones and cut the characters to be printed into the stone. The stone was covered with ink and the paper was then pressed on top. The result was sort of a "negative" print because the ink filled in the background and the characters came out white.

print many copies of the same document. When it came time to print a different document, he heated the tray over a fire to get the wax to melt again. Once the wax became soft, he reset the letters for the new document and got ready to print again. By reusing the same letters, he saved a tremendous amount of time and effort.

IMPACT   By the mid 1400s, printers in Europe were experimenting, trying to improve on these techniques while using different materials. After working in secret for almost 20 years, in 1448 a German printer in the town of Mainz unveiled a system that was destined to change history. This system, which revolutionized the way printing was done, was developed by Johannes Gensefleisch, but most people know him by his mother's family name, Gutenberg!

CHILDREN OF THIS INVENTION   Once printers adopted the Gutenberg system, books and newspapers became common. Most important, for the first time, people could easily exchange information, and knowledge flowed freely to any member of society who could read.

An expert in metalwork, Gutenberg developed a new metal alloy from which he could make individual pieces of type. These pieces could then be set into a wooden frame called a typestick. Each typestick would then be locked into a larger frame, which was placed into a press that was similar to the device used for squeezing grapes in wine making. Using this system, several hundred copies of an entire book could be printed in a few short weeks.

THE CLOCK

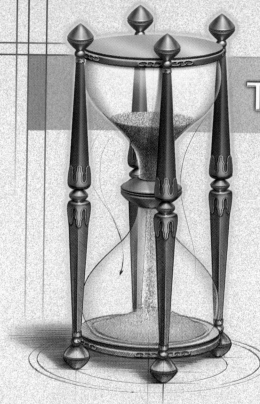

In the first century A.D., the Romans came up with a concept similar to the Egyptian water clock, except they used sand instead of water. Both of these devices were useful for counting how quickly time passed, but you couldn't use them to tell what time it really was.

In early hunting/gathering societies there really wasn't any need to tell time. People usually got up at dawn, ate when they were hungry, and went to sleep when it got dark. Later, as people began to plant crops and herd animals, they learned to measure the length of the day by watching the Sun as it moved across the sky. By 3500 B.C., simple sundials were used throughout the Middle East to measure the passage of daylight hours, but it wasn't until people began to travel and explore that they needed ways of measuring time that stayed constant. In other words, they needed a clock that ran whether the Sun was out or not.

The first attempt at measuring time without looking to the sky can be traced to about 1400 B.C. when ancient Egyptians used simple water clocks. Water trickled through a hole in the bottom of a bowl that had markings on the inside. As the water level in the bowl dropped, a set amount of time could be counted.

HOW IT WORKS   The first true clock appears to have been created in China in the year 1088. This unique device was powered by water falling into a series of cups attached to a waterwheel. Every 15 minutes, one cup would fill up and the weight of the water would turn the wheel. While this mechanism was probably not the most accurate, it was kept running for more than 300 years.

IMPACT   These simple clocks were only accurate to within an hour each day, and they had to be checked regularly with a sundial. As the mechanisms became more sophisticated, people started depending on clocks to manage their days.

Businesses opened and closed at certain hours, official meeting times were set, and gradually people began to synchronize their actions with one another.

CHILDREN OF THIS INVENTION Weight-driven clocks remained the standard until 1657, when Dutch inventor Christian Huygens came up with the idea of using a heavy pendulum swinging back and forth to drive the clock.

This same type of mechanism is still used today in many grandfather clocks. Later, as metals became more refined, clock makers were able to switch to spring-driven clocks. Unlike pendulum clocks, spring-driven clocks could be moved from one place to another without disrupting the mechanism. This allowed navigators aboard ships to begin to use clocks to time their progress and measure their location far out at sea, further opening the world for greater exploration.

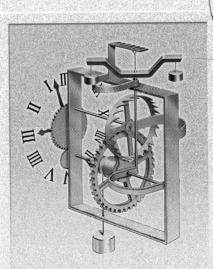

The first mechanical clocks were developed in Europe around 1300. Instead of flowing water or sand, they were driven by a weight that was tied to the end of a cord. As the weight slowly fell, the cord turned a shaft, which in turn moved the hands of the clock. To wind the clock, the weight was brought back up to the top of the chamber and gravity would start the process again.

BLACK POWDER AND THE CHEMICAL REVOLUTION

With the smelting of bronze, iron, and steel, people discovered that they could modify raw materials, changing their properties to fit their needs. By mixing different substances together and treating them with heat, water, and other chemicals, they found that they could make a whole variety of new materials with many unusual properties. Black powder, which was used in early guns and explosives, is thought to be a Chinese invention, since it was used extensively in fireworks by as early as A.D. 900. The first written recipe for making black powder is found in an A.D. 1044 book by Wu Ching Tsao, although he certainly was not the inventor.

HOW IT WORKS Black powder is really a combination of three naturally occurring chemicals: charcoal (which makes it black), sulfur, and potassium nitrate, which is a salt commonly called saltpeter. When mixed in the

The first description of black powder being used as a weapon comes from about A.D. 1125, when it was packed tightly into iron pots and set off with a fuse. These primitive bombs not only scared the enemy but made the use of armor obsolete.

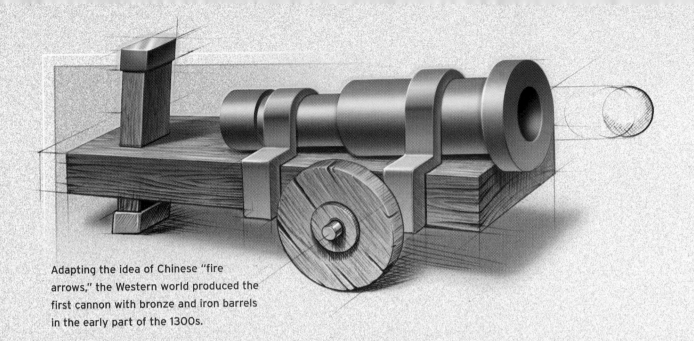

Adapting the idea of Chinese "fire arrows," the Western world produced the first cannon with bronze and iron barrels in the early part of the 1300s.

right combinations and set on fire, this material burns extremely fast, releasing a great deal of smoke and hot gas.

IMPACT The first record of black powder use was not as a weapon of war, but as a material that was thrown into fires to produce big flames during different ceremonies. Once people learned how effective black powder was as a weapon, they purposely began to invent new uses for it in warfare. The first guns were really a type of rocket used in 1232 by the Chinese in a war against the Mongols. These "fire arrows" were simply bamboo tubes reinforced with iron straps, sealed on one end, and packed with black powder. In launching fire arrows and similar missiles toward the enemy, they often killed many of their own users because the weapons frequently blew up when launched.

CHILDREN OF THIS INVENTION Once cannons were introduced, it was only a short hop to other types of firearms that not only changed the way war was fought, but also changed the entire balance of power in the world. As one medieval passage put it: "Gunpowder killed both knight and serf and proved them both equal." It's an unfortunate fact of life that some of the most important technological revolutions come out of humans' desire to wage war better, and gunpowder is no exception. Much later on, gunpowder and the explosives based on it would lead to the first rockets that would ultimately propel humans into space. Another practical invention that came from the use of gunpowder was the match!

THE MAGNETIC COMPASS

Humans love to explore. From the earliest time, people have always been curious about what's "out there" beyond their local area. The problem with exploring new territories is that once you leave your local neighborhood, there are no familiar landmarks to help you get back home again. In ancient Egypt, China, and Babylonia, people learned that they could navigate around the earth by using the position of the sun and stars in the sky. The problem was that the stars in the sky could help you only if they were visible. If it was cloudy, you were out of luck!

As far back as 600 B.C., both Greek and Chinese philosophers knew that a certain heavy black rock exhibited strange attractive powers when it was brought near a piece of iron. Know as magnetite or lodestone, these natural magnets were turned into the first compasses. By 1100 A.D., the Chinese had learned to make magnets by rubbing a small piece of iron against a lodestone until the iron also became magnetic. One of the first uses of these manufactured magnets was in a "floating compass." A superthin piece of iron was shaped like a fish and magnetized. Then the iron fish was floated in a bowl of water where it would swing around until its head pointed north.

As long ago as 500 B.C., Chinese miners used the magnetic properties of lodestone to point the way. Taking a piece of this natural magnet and carving it into the shape of a spoon, they made a device called a *sinan*. The sinan was placed on a flat surface and the handle of the spoon would slowly swing around until it pointed north. They probably didn't know it at the time, but this unique device was the world's first magnetic compass.

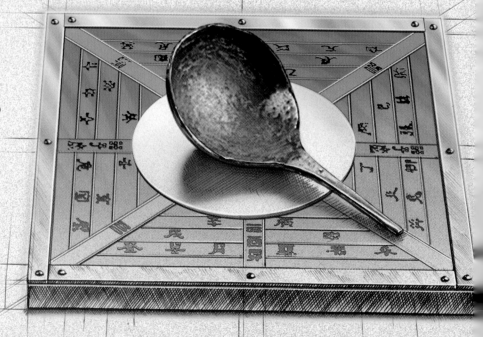

HOW IT WORKS   A compass works because of a basic rule of science called the law of poles. Every magnet regardless of its shape has two distinct ends, or poles. When the north pole of one is brought near the south pole of another, they attract. As it turns out, because of fluid action deep within the earth, our planet acts like a giant magnet with north and south poles. When a compass needle (which is really a tiny magnet) is allowed to swing freely, its south end points to Earth's magnetic north pole.

A simple floating compass was tough to use out at sea or when traveling over rough roads. To solve the problem of the pointer bouncing around, the compass needle was fixed with a pin in the center of a glass-covered brass case. (Brass is nonmagnetic, so it doesn't attract the magnetized needle.) As long as the compass was held flat, the needle would point in the right direction.

IMPACT   Until the compass was developed, overcast skies of fall and winter often kept entire fleets tied up at dock for fear of getting lost at sea. On the open water, without the sun to sight on in the day or the stars at night, navigators lost all sense of direction. With a primitive compass as a backup, traders were able to sail year-round and explorers dared to try new routes. With the compass needle to guide them, explorers began to "boldly go where no man had gone before," crossing large sections of uncharted ocean, opening up new worlds that led to even greater discoveries.

CHILDREN OF THIS INVENTION   Over the years, explorers discovered another problem with the magnetic compass. As it turns out, the earth has two north poles! One is magnetic north, while the other is geographic, or true, north.

These two poles are *not* in the same place, but are separated by several hundred miles. As a result, when you read a compass, you always have to adjust, or declinate, your compass to allow for the difference between the two. Sailors slowly figured this out and by the late 1400s, declination charts were in constant use.

THE MICROSCOPE

It's hard to imagine a world without cells, bacteria, and viruses, yet before the early 1600s, not one of these things was known to exist, simply because they're all too small to be seen with the naked eye. This all changed in 1590 when Dutch lens maker Hans Janssen and his son Zacharias placed two lenses on top of each other, which greatly increased the apparent size of the object they were looking at. They didn't know it at the time, but they had stumbled on an invention that would open up a whole new world—the world of the microscope.

This is a drawing of Robert Hooke's compound microscope that used two lenses in the main viewing tube to magnify an object. The object was lit by a beam of light from the flame of an oil lamp that was focused at the bottom of the microscope.

HOW IT WORKS   Long before the Janssens came up with the microscope, people knew that curved pieces of glass and clear crystals could make objects appear larger. These simple magnifiers worked on the principle of refraction, or the bending of light, and by the early 1500s, they were common throughout Europe.

The compound microscope, which uses two lenses separated by a short distance, increases the image of an object many times more than a simple magnifier because the second lens multiplies the magnification of the first. For the Janssens, the microscope was simply a curiosity, but for Robert Hooke and Antonie van Leeuwenhoek, it led to a new area of science called *microbiology.*

IMPACT   Robert Hooke was born in 1635 on the Isle of Wight in England and was a contemporary of Isaac Newton. In his spare time, Hooke used the microscope to make thousands of observations of things like snowflakes, insect eyes, and parts of plants. He was the first one to use the term *cell* as a building block of living things, and he published his findings along with many drawings in a book called *Micrographia* in 1665.

While Hooke was working in England, Antonie van Leeuwenhoek was busy in Holland. In his spare time, he learned how to grind lenses and developed a technique for making extremely high-powered, single-lens microscopes. In 1674, he developed a device that could magnify an object 250 times, and with it he was the first person on record to observe "very little animalcules," which were really microscopic organisms living in rainwater, pond water, and even the human mouth.

Today, we call van Leeuwenhoek's animalcules *protozoa*, simple microscopic life-forms that live in many places in the environment. For more than 50 years, van Leeuwenhoek used his magnifiers to break new ground, being the first to observe red blood cells, see flea eggs (which proved that they did not grow from the sand, as some people had thought), and do a detailed study on the anatomy of the ant.

CHILDREN OF THIS INVENTION

Based on the work of Hooke and van Leeuwenhoek, other scientists like Louis Pasteur would be able to identify the causes of many diseases, which in turn led to the development of antiseptics and antibiotics.

Using microscopes, scientists and doctors can not only see microorganisms like protozoa, but also see individual cells like the red blood cells seen here.

THE TELESCOPE

Many books give credit for the invention of the telescope to Galileo Galilei, one of the greatest scientists who ever lived. While Galileo may have been the first to turn the telescope to the stars, he actually "borrowed" the idea from Hans Lippershay, an eyeglass maker who, like van Leeuwenhoek (see "The Microscope"), lived in Holland.

HOW IT WORKS   Realizing that the discovery could be put to practical use, Lippershay used glue to mount two lenses inside a hollow wooden tube and called it the *kijker*, which is Dutch for "looker." This primitive telescope was an immediate success, but not for scientific purposes.

This drawing shows the type of telescope Galileo used to make his discoveries. The observing tube had a convex front lens and a concave eyepiece lens. While this type of device allowed people to see distant objects "up close," the objects were often quite blurry. Over time, many scientists worked to improve the quality of telescope lenses to produce the sharp, clear images we have today.

Both the Dutch government and the king of France wanted telescopes because they could be used for military purposes. Using telescopes, soldiers could see enemy forces while they were still far out at sea. By giving a land-based army a half-day's warning, the telescope made it impossible to get caught by a sneak attack from the sea!

While Lippershay is often given sole credit for inventing the telescope, it is believed that a number of different lens makers living in Holland at about the same time had also discovered how to assemble a device that would make a distant object appear closer. This idea is supported by the fact that Lippershay was turned down by the Dutch government for a patent because his device was already considered to be "common knowledge."

IMPACT   While telescopes had their military importance, it was as a scientific tool that they had their greatest impact. Being a man of science, Galileo was always on the lookout for new devices with which he could observe the world around him. While traveling through Venice, Italy, in 1609, Galileo learned about the "looker" and immediately set off to build one. Using a better set of lenses, he built a refracting telescope that could magnify objects more than 30 times. Pointing it to the sky, Galileo would not only be the first person to get a close-up look at the Moon, Jupiter, and the Sun (which eventually cost him his eyesight), but he would also make discoveries that would change forever how we as humans viewed our place in the universe.

Until Galileo's time, people believed that Earth was the center of the universe and everything, including the Sun, Moon, stars, and planets, revolved around us. In 1543, a Polish astronomer named Nicolaus Copernicus challenged this idea by suggesting that Earth and the other planets went around the Sun instead. Many people had a hard time accepting the Copernican system, but by using his telescope, Galileo made a series of observations that strongly supported it.

CHILDREN OF THIS INVENTION   Today, telescopes are looking farther and deeper into the heavens, seeing not only the birth of new stars, but closing in on the birth of the universe itself. Each day, astronomers use these devices to push the limits of time and space farther away, and while the numbers can sometimes be mind-boggling, it's important to remember that the revolution that rocked the world started less than 400 years ago!

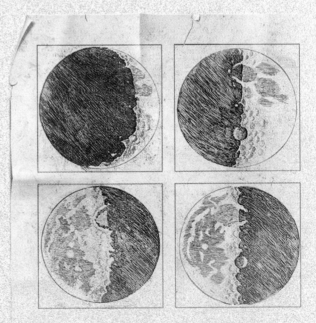

In 1610, Galileo published his telescopic observations in a book called *The Starry Messenger*. In it, he included these drawings of the Moon showing that it was not smooth, but marked by craters and mountains.

THE STEAM ENGINE

B y the late 1600s, explorers had charted most of the oceans and trade between Asia, Europe, Africa, and the Americas was commonplace. Despite all this progress, industrial technologies were limited in how much they could grow because they still depended on natural power sources like wind, water, animals, and humans. This was all about to change because of a simple device patented by an English engineer named Thomas Savery in 1698.

HOW IT WORKS Learning of the constant problems that miners faced in trying to drain their mines of unwanted water, Savery set to work building a new type of pump that worked using pressure created by steam. In his system, steam from a boiler was piped into a tank filled with water. The steam in the tank was then allowed to condense, which created a vacuum inside the tank. A pipe leading to the water in the mine was connected to the tank, so the vacuum "sucked" up the water out of the mine and into the tank. Unfortunately for Savery, his "fire engine" was not very efficient, but it opened the door for other inventors to step through.

Thomas Newcomen was also busy working on the miners' problem, and in 1712, he installed his first engine. Instead of using high-pressure steam like Savery, Newcomen used steam at normal atmospheric pressure (like the steam coming out of a tea kettle when it's boiling). This simple change not only made his engine more efficient, but safer to operate, too. For close to 50 years, his steam engine was the best available until Scottish engineer James Watt tackled the problem.

IMPACT When people hear the name Watt, they usually think of electricity (as in a 100-watt lightbulb), but the man for whom this unit of power is named built his reputation on the steam engine. Watt's first encounter with a steam engine came when he was working as a technician at Glasgow University in 1764. He started modifying the device, and in May 1765 he came up with a truly practical and efficient steam engine.

Because of Watt's steam engine, factories and mills no longer had to be located near streams to power them. All you needed was a small amount of water and a fire to boil it. As a result, new cities started springing up near coal and iron deposits. Over the next 25 years, Watt would continue to perfect the engine that helped to power the Industrial Revolution.

CHILDREN OF THIS INVENTION   As steam engines became more efficient, their mobility gave transportation engineers a new tool to work with. In 1802, in Scotland, William Symington built the first steam-powered tugboat, which quickly gave rise to Robert Fulton's steamboat in 1807. In 1803, English engineer Richard Trevithick started experimenting with the design of a steam-powered carriage. This device was perfected by George Stephenson, who in 1829 introduced the "Rocket," the first commercial railroad engine.

Unlike the Savery fire engine, the Newcomen engine didn't pump water directly. Instead, on top was a large wooden lever that was pivoted in the middle like a giant seesaw. One end of the beam was hooked up to a pump via a chain, and the other end was connected to a big piston that was placed inside a cylinder right above the boiler. When steam entered the bottom of the cylinder, it pushed up on the piston, which pushed up on one end of the lever. Once the piston reached as high as it could go, cold water was sprayed on the cylinder. The cold water condensed the steam back to a liquid, and the piston quickly fell. The cycle started again when the next burst of steam was sent into the cylinder.

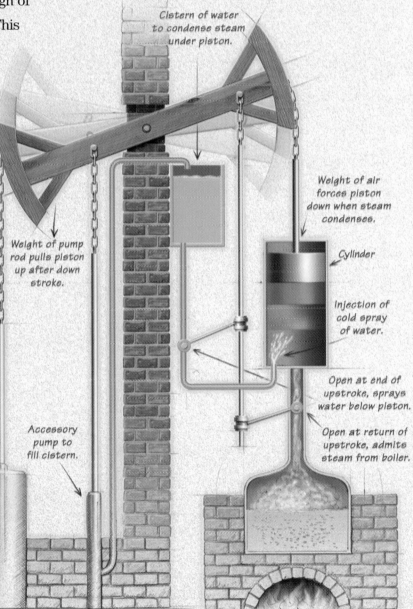

Cistern of water to condense steam under piston.

Weight of air forces piston down when steam condenses.

Cylinder

Injection of cold spray of water.

Weight of pump rod pulls piston up after down stroke.

Open at end of upstroke, sprays water below piston.

Open at return of upstroke, admits steam from boiler.

Accessory pump to fill cistern.

chapter four

THE AGE OF

ELECTRICITY AND

COMMUNICATION

1799 – 1887

BY THE LATE 1700s, the Industrial Revolution was in full swing, and once again, lifestyles were changing. Factories became the workplace for millions, and steam was rapidly replacing water and wind as the primary source of power. As cities grew, problems and populations skyrocketed. Shortages of clean drinking water were commonplace, and the disposal of garbage and sewage became major issues. After a series of plagues killed millions, public health became a major concern, and the medical arts began receiving a great deal of attention.

Spurred on by the work of Galileo, Newton, Hooke, and van Leeuwenhoek, scientists working in universities began making new discoveries at an incredible pace. Using the microscope, telescope, and a variety of other instruments, they were pushing the limits of knowledge further each day. As the nineteenth century progressed, a new communications revolution was under way, this time powered by the electron!

THE BATTERY

Today, it's hard to imagine a world without electricity. We use it for almost everything, including lighting, writing, cleaning, preening, cooking, and even looking (at movies and television). In fact, electricity has become such a critical part of our society that whenever we experience a temporary power failure, it seems as if the entire world grinds to a halt.

Humans had known about electricity for a long time. As early as 600 B.C., people had discovered that you could get electrical charges on certain materials when you rubbed them. This type of electricity, called static, was an interesting phenomenon, but it wasn't very useful. What runs almost every electrical device today is something called current, or flowing electricity. The first person to tap into this source was Alessandro Volta, but he based his work on the discoveries of a fellow scientist named Luigi Galvani.

HOW IT WORKS   Galvani's specialty was anatomy, and while dissecting a dead frog one day, he noticed that the leg twitched whenever it was given a large static shock. Galvani was convinced that the reason the leg moved was some type of "animal electricity." He began testing other materials and discovered that by simply placing a frog's leg on a copper hook and hanging it on an iron railing, he could get the same reaction as with the static charge.

In 1791, Galvani's findings were published and Volta read them. Volta was convinced that the electricity did not come from the frog but came from the two metals acting to create a simple circuit. He argued that the frog-leg twitch only showed the result of the flowing electricity and was not the cause of it. In 1794, Volta conducted experiments by placing different metals in salt solutions, and, in 1800, he finally met with success.

IMPACT Volta's battery not only proved that electricity could be generated without having to rub two objects together, but it was also the first source of continuous, or current, electricity. This meant that in addition to steam, people had a new, clean power source that they could tap anytime they wanted. In no time at all, other scientists and inventors started using batteries in their experiments. In the following 30 years there was a virtual explosion of battery powered devices.

CHILDREN OF THIS INVENTION

Batteries led directly to the invention of many important devices, including the electromagnet, the electric motor, the electric heater, electric arc lights, and later, the telegraph and telephone. Today, high-powered, rechargeable batteries are used in hundreds of different portable electric devices ranging from cell phones and laptop computers to the emergency medical equipment carried on ambulances.

By trial and error, Volta found that if he took copper and zinc discs and stacked them up in alternating layers separated by pieces of cloth soaked in brine (salt water), he could generate a continuous flow of electricity. His invention was called the Voltaic Pile, and it was the first electric battery.

ANESTHESIA

This early inhaler was used to give patients ether before surgery. The cloth in the bottle was soaked with liquid and the gas would travel through the tube up to the face mask.

Have you ever had to go to the dentist to have a cavity filled? In most cases, they give you a simple shot of novocaine, and presto, the pain goes away. Novocaine and drugs like it are called anesthetics. Not only have they made life in a dentist chair bearable, but they have also made modern surgery a reality.

Before the mid-1800s, there were very few drugs available that would block pain. Certain drugs that made people sleepy, like opium, henbane, and alcohol, were tried, but frequently, when these were given to people before an operation, the drug itself would wind up killing them. More often than not, when a doctor had to do surgery, he or she would simply tie the person down and operate without giving the patient anything to block the pain.

During wartime, when wounded soldiers needed to have emergency amputations, the surgeon would give them something to bite on, like a bullet or a wad of bandage. This particularly crude way of dealing with pain became known as "biting the bullet," an expression that is still used today. As you might suspect, given the option, most people chose *not* to have surgery done, even if it meant that they would face certain death! This all changed, though, in 1799, when Humphry Davy, a 21-year-old chemist working at the Pneumatic Institute in Clifton, England, discovered nitrous oxide.

HOW IT WORKS Nitrous oxide, which is more commonly called laughing gas, was just one of many different compounds Davy tested. His procedure was simple. He would mix up a chemical compound, breathe it in, and see what happened. This type of procedure would never be used today by scientists. In doing his experiments, Davy almost killed himself on several occasions, but he did learn that nitrous oxide would block pain.

IMPACT   Chemists began to investigate other compounds. In 1842, a chemistry student named William Clark used ethyl ether on a woman who was about to have a tooth removed. Later that same year, Crawford Long, a surgeon from Jefferson, Georgia, began using ether regularly in his operations.

CHILDREN OF THIS INVENTION   Today, there are many types of anesthetics available. Some are general anesthetics because they work on the entire body, making a person unconscious. For smaller operations and tooth extractions, doctors usually use a local anesthetic, which simply deadens the pain around the location of the operation for a few hours. So, next time you have to go to the dentist, have no fear. Just ask for novocaine and everything should be fine—that is, unless your dentist hands you a bullet to bite on!

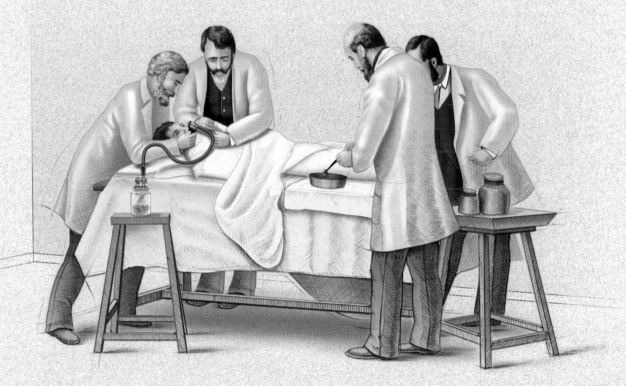

The first true public test of ethyl ether came in October 1846, when an American dentist named William Morton working at Massachusetts General Hospital used it successfully to remove a neck tumor from a woman in Boston. The doctors attending the operation were so impressed that by the end of the decade the use of ether, nitrous oxide, and other compounds such as chloroform became a common practice.

PHOTOGRAPHY

Today, photography is a breeze. Just point the camera, press the button, and almost instantly, you have a perfect copy of the scene that you're looking at. Before the invention of the camera, artists had to work for hours to try to capture an image. No matter how objective they tried to be, their drawings could never be perfect copies.

Photography was made possible because of all the experimenting people were doing with chemicals in the late 1700s. One critical discovery was made by J. H. Schulze. Schulze noticed that certain compounds containing silver salts would get darker after they had been left out in a bright light. This seemingly minor reaction would ultimately be the key to modern photography.

HOW IT WORKS The first step in taking a photograph is gathering the light from the scene to be captured. As early as 1600, people had discovered how lenses could be used to direct and focus light, and a device called the *camera obscura*, which is

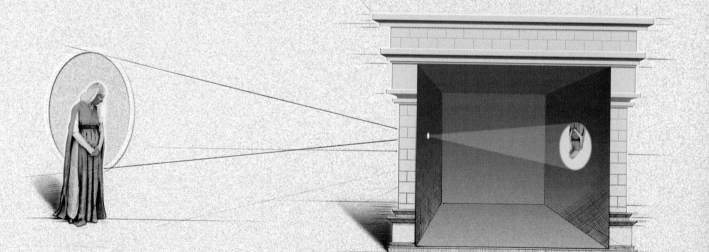

The first *camera obscuras* were simply dark rooms with a small hole in one wall. As light entered the hole, it refracted, or bent a little, and cast a perfect upside-down image of what was outside on the wall opposite the hole. Artists found them helpful for tracing scenes and portraits of people. Substituting a sheet of paper for the screen, they could copy an image directly from the light.

Latin for "chamber of dark," had been invented. By 1816, all the elements were in place for a true "photographic" camera to be developed, and a French inventor named Joseph Nicéphore Niepce put the pieces together.

Learning of Schulze's discovery, Niepce took a metal plate made of pewter and coated it with different silver compounds. After many hours in the sun, a *heliograph*, or "sun drawing," appeared. Convinced that he was on the right track, he substituted paper covered with silver chloride for the pewter and loaded the paper in the back of a portable *camera obscura*. Using this method, he was able to get a crude image of a scene from outside his workroom on the paper. Unfortunately, the image quickly faded, but the first official photograph or "light drawing" was taken.

Building on the work done by Joseph Niepce, Louis Daguerre greatly improved the process of photography. He introduced the daguerreotype camera in Paris in 1839. It was the standard for almost 30 years.

IMPACT   By the late 1820s, Niepce and his heliographs were making quite a stir around France. At that same time, Louis Daguerre, a French painter who had also been working with "fixing light," learned about his work. He convinced the financially strapped Niepce to go into partnership in 1829. Niepce died suddenly in 1833, and Daguerre took over the business and is usually credited as the inventor of photography.

With a photograph, people could finally record an exact duplicate of what the eye saw. No longer did the world have to depend on the artist's eye to capture an event or image. By the mid-1800s, cameras had improved so much that photojournalists like Mathew Brady were using them not only to make portraits, but record historical events and show people the true horrors of war.

CHILDREN OF THIS INVENTION   In 1874, George Eastman came up with a process using light-sensitive chemicals fixed on long strips of dry paper to make prints. He later improved this technique by using a new synthetic material called "celluloid," and modern photographic film was born.

THE ELECTRIC MOTOR

Today, electric motors can be found in hundreds of appliances, including blenders, refrigerators, washing machines, and clocks. It's hard to imagine getting through a day without these devices, but before the mid-1800s, electric motors did not exist. Like so many inventions, the electric motor came from a simple scientific discovery.

Once batteries became available in the early 1800s, scientists began experimenting with the many things that current electricity could do. In 1819, a Danish schoolteacher named Hans Christian Oersted was demonstrating a battery for one of his classes when he noticed that each time he connected it to a wire, the needle on a compass that was on a desk nearby would spin. For years, scientists thought that there had to be a connection between electricity and magnetism, and Oersted found it. The device he invented became known as the electromagnet, and it's what makes an electric motor work.

HOW IT WORKS   The key to making an electric motor spin has to do with the law of poles. The north pole of one magnet will always seek the south pole of another magnet. If two of

Stator

Rotar

Stator

A motor has a series of fixed bar magnets called stators around the sides of a chamber and an electromagnet mounted on a shaft in the middle of the chamber. This electromagnet is called a *rotar* because as the current flows through it, its poles are attracted to the poles of the bar magnets, making it rotate. By changing the direction of current flow every half turn, the rotar keeps spinning.

the same poles are brought together, they will repel each other. When electricity flows through the coil of an electromagnet, the direction in which the electricity flows will control the direction of the poles. By reversing the direction of the electricity, you will reverse the polarity of the electromagnet.

In 1821, English chemist Michael Faraday took a bar magnet and placed it straight up and down in a bowl of liquid mercury. He suspended a wire from a metal hook above the

In 1831, Faraday took a permanent bar magnet and moved it past a coil of wire. In this way he was able to induce a current of electricity in the coil. What Faraday had come up with was the first electric generator, which Thomas Edison would use 50 years later to light up the streets of New York.

bowl and allowed the end of the wire to touch the mercury. When he connected a battery between the top of the hook and the bowl of mercury, the wire began to rotate. This was the world's first electric motor.

IMPACT While Faraday's experiment proved that electric motors could work, the real breakthrough came in 1835 in America, where Joseph Henry invented the commutator. This clever device kept reversing the direction of current flow in the rotar without having to disconnect the battery, which made the electric motor more efficient and practical. Within a few short years, electric motors were being used to run all sorts of factory equipment, replacing hand cranks and steam engines. Later, they were introduced into the home through a whole host of kitchen appliances that we still depend on today.

CHILDREN OF THIS INVENTION While they were doing their experiments with motors, both Henry and Faraday made another discovery concerning electricity and magnets. Called electromagnetic induction, it's what makes generators produce electricity.

THE TELEGRAPH

This complex telegraph system used six wires to transmit a message. By turning on different switches, the operator at one end would cause an electric current to flow through different wires. The electric current would activate electromagnets under the panel at the receiver, which would cause the different needles on top to point to the proper letter.

Since the dawn of speech, the ability of humans to communicate over a long distance has always been limited by one simple factor—how loud a person could yell! Using your voice alone, the best you can do is maybe a few hundred yards (meters). Sending a message over a large distance instantaneously is not a new idea. For thousands of years, people used many ingenious ways of doing it. They tried everything from smoke signals and beating drums to waving flags and placing lanterns in church steeples! While all these methods worked to some degree, they were all limited in the distance they could span. With the invention of the battery and electromagnet, this all changed.

In 1832 in Munich, Germany, Baron Schilling, a diplomat working in the Russian embassy, was able to demonstrate a simple system in which a magnetic needle suspended over a coil of wire would twitch back and forth when an electric signal was sent through the wire. While this simple setup was a far cry from the wireless cell phones we have today, it proved that long-distance communication using electricity was possible, and the race was on to build the first true telegraph.

HOW IT WORKS In 1836, English engineer William Cooke used the principles laid out by Baron Schilling to build the first commercial electromagnetic telegraph. Consulting first with Michael Faraday, and then enlisting the aid of Professor Charles Wheatstone of Kings College, Cooke designed a detector using five different electromagnetic needles.

IMPACT   The Cooke and Wheatstone telegraph was used in England by railroads to signal the arrival of trains for about 10 years, and by 1852, the two had installed more than 4,000 miles (6,400 km) of telegraph cable. Unfortunately, because it was difficult to use and costly to install, this system didn't have a major impact. The real breakthrough in telegraphy was made by an American painter whose name was destined to become synonymous with the telegraph.

In 1832, Samuel F. B. Morse was sailing home from England when he struck up a conversation with two passengers about the recently discovered electromagnet. Morse was intrigued with the device and by the end of the trip, he had worked out the designs for a basic electromagnetic telegraph.

While Morse certainly didn't invent the telegraph, his system and code was the one that was most widely used and truly revolutionized the world of communication. With financial support from Congress, Morse set up his first long-distance telegraph line from Washington, D.C., to Baltimore. On May 24, 1844, he typed the message "What hath God wrought?" The answer was instantaneous—long-distance communications!

CHILDREN OF THIS INVENTION   In later years, other inventors like Thomas Edison and Alexander Graham Bell would get their start working on improving the telegraph, and this simple device would eventually evolve into the telephone, the stock ticker, and the radio.

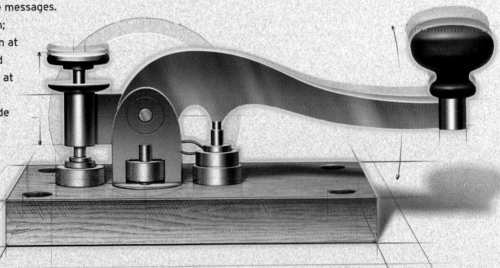

In 1838, Morse came up with a simple telegraph key to send the messages. The key acted as a switch; when it was pressed down at one end, electricity would flow to an electromagnet at the other end that would click. By developing a code consisting of differently spaced clicks (dots and dashes), Morse could tap out a message of any length over any distance.

CHEMICAL FERTILIZERS

Anyone who has ever planted a garden knows the benefits of fertilizer. With just a little sprinkle, you can get award-winning tomatoes, potatoes, and even zucchini. In ancient times, there were no such things as fertilizers, but being careful observers of nature, people figured out a few tricks to help their gardens grow.

By around 200 B.C., the Roman philosopher Cato recommended that if farmers added manure to the soil, rotated their crops (planted a different crop each year), and added lime, they would produce a greater amount of growth. People had no clue why these things worked, but since they did work, these and other "organic" means of farming became the standard practice.

By the mid-1700s, scientists were starting to get a handle on different chemicals and understand how they worked to make plants grow. In 1813, Sir Humphry Davy published *Elements of Agricultural Chemistry*, in which he suggested that certain chemicals might be added to encourage plant growth. The real breakthrough came in Germany in 1838, when a man named Justus von Liebig laid down the law.

A farmer from the 1900s dumping manure from a cart into a field. Even though they didn't know why it worked, farmers knew that spreading manure on their fields helped to make crops grow better. Even today, many farmers use composted manure as an organic fertilizer.

HOW IT WORKS   Justus von Liebig was a chemist working as a professor at the University of Giessen, where he set up one of the most advanced labs of the day. Drawing on the work of Humphry Davy, von Liebig determined that the reason specific materials helped plants grow was that they were made up of certain "essential elements."

In 1840, he published *Organic Chemistry in Its Application to Agriculture and Physiology*, in which he not only presented his findings, but spelled out what has become know as "Liebig's Law." Also called "the law of the minimum," it states that an organism's growth would be limited by the element present in least amounts relative to its needs. What this means is that in order to make plants grow really well, you have to give them a wide variety of nutrients in just the right mixture.

Modern chemistry has allowed for the production of fertilizers that have the exact balance of essential elements needed by different types of plants.

IMPACT   As a result of using von Liebig's recommendations, within a few short years productivity almost doubled in some places, and fewer farmers could now produce more food for more people. This not only helped to transform farming into a high-tech industry, but it freed up more labor to work in factories, which in turn fueled the Industrial Revolution.

CHILDREN OF THIS INVENTION   The work done by Justus von Liebig helped to promote other areas of organic chemistry, which eventually led to the development of synthetic materials like plastics. In addition, his work with plants set the stage for current breakthroughs in genetic engineering.

THE INTERNAL COMBUSTION ENGINE

It's hard to imagine a world without cars, trucks, motorcycles, airplanes, or powerboats. All of these modern marvels of engineering help transport us and our goods from one place to another, but none of them would be possible if it weren't for the internal combustion engine. While the steam engine brought a revolution in industry, the internal combustion engine put people on the move!

As the name suggests, an internal combustion engine is different from a steam engine because all of the burning of the fuel happens inside the engine itself. A steam engine is an example of an external combustion engine because a fuel like coal or wood is burned in an outside boiler, which then heats water to make steam to push a piston. This multistep process requires a very large engine that consumes a great deal of fuel, and while it's good for factories and for large ships and trains, it's impractical for personal vehicles. Individuals of the world had to wait until 1878 to get moving. That's when German engineer Nikolaus Otto came up with a better way of pushing a piston.

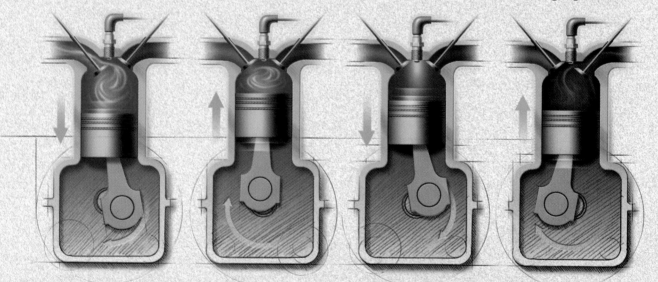

A four-stroke engine uses four separate movements of the piston in the cylinder to get the necessary power. In the first stroke, the piston moves down, creating a vacuum, which sucks the air/fuel mixture into the cylinder through a valve at the top of the chamber. In the second stroke, the valve closes and the piston moves up, compressing the mixture in the cylinder. When maximum compression is reached, a spark plug at the top of the cylinder fires, causing the air/fuel mixture to explode. This forces the piston back down, creating the "power stroke." Finally, on the fourth stroke, the piston moves up again, and another valve at the top of the cylinder opens to let the exhaust gas out. The cycle then starts again.

HOW IT WORKS　The idea of an internal combustion engine can be traced back to 1680, when the Dutch scientist Christian Huygens designed a piston-driven engine that used gunpowder as the fuel. While this may have been an explosive idea, as you can imagine, it had some serious drawbacks! A much more practical idea was offered in 1862, when a Frenchman named Alphonse Beau de Rochas suggested that you could get power by compressing a flammable gas in a cylinder first, then igniting the fuel. This idea was also adapted by Nikolaus Otto. In 1876, Otto designed the four-stroke engine, which would take the world by storm. Otto took out a patent for his idea in 1876, but because it was similar in concept to the one that Rochas described in the 1860s, his application was denied. Even so, Otto started building engines that were used in factories all over Europe. By 1900, almost a quarter of a million were in existence.

This is a drawing of the first motorcar. In early 1885, Karl Benz began experimenting with putting lightweight four-stroke engines into carriages, and the automobile was born. Within a few short years, other engineers, including Gottlieb Daimler (who worked with Otto) and Rudolf Diesel, began reworking the engines to make them faster, lighter, more powerful, and more efficient.

IMPACT　Since it was a small, compact power plant, the four-stroke engine rapidly found its way into many different uses, including running farm machinery and vehicles. Because of it, the first true motorcars came into existence.

CHILDREN OF THIS INVENTION　By 1898, automobile manufacturing had spread from Europe across the sea, with 50 different companies building cars in the United States alone. At about the same time, the first speedboats and motorcycles were developed. Finally, in 1903, the internal combustion engine took to the skies when the Wright brothers used one to power their first airplane!

ANTISEPTICS

Lister adapted a method used to clean up bad-smelling sewers in London. In 1875, he developed a device that sprayed carbolic acid in the operating room to kill the unseen germs.

I magine this for a moment: After weeks of sore throats, your doctor finally decides that it's time for you to have your tonsils out. No big deal, thousands of people get it done every year. You check into the hospital, and you go into the operating room and lie down on the table. All the doctors and nurses are standing there, but something is seriously wrong. They're not wearing sterile clothes, masks, or gloves. Worse still, the surgeon, who has been working on another patient in the room at the same time, takes the same scalpel he's been using and without even rinsing it off, is about to use it on you! While this sounds like something out of a horror movie, in the 1850s it was a scene that happened in hospitals every day.

In the mid-1800s, even having simple surgery was a life-threatening situation. Most doctors believed that what you couldn't see wouldn't hurt you. People didn't know about germs because they couldn't see them. This all changed with the work of an English doctor named Joseph Lister, who not only had a famous mouthwash named after him but also significantly changed the way medicine was practiced.

HOW IT WORKS   In 1861, Lister was offered the chance to head up a new surgical wing at the Glasgow Royal Infirmary, and it was here that he would make his greatest impact, but not as a surgeon.

When Lister took over, the leading cause of death in the hospital was not from the surgery itself, but from *sepsis* or "hospital fever," a strange disease that often followed successful surgery and killed almost half of the people who had operations. For some time, doctors had thought that "bad air" was the cause of this ailment, but Lister was convinced that there was another carrier at play. Drawing on his knowledge of the microscope and the work of Louis Pasteur, who five years earlier had shown that wine fermented because of invisible microorganisms, Lister started his war on germs. Many other doctors thought he was crazy.

In August 1865, a boy named James Greenlees was brought to the hospital with a broken shin, an injury that frequently led to sepsis and death. Lister set the fracture and treated the wound with bandages soaked in carbolic acid. Six weeks later, young James walked out of the hospital completely healed, and the world began to take Lister seriously.

Even though these bacteria are invisible to the naked eye, they are responsible for causing severe infection and even death if they get into an open wound.

IMPACT   Lister called his technique *antisepsis*, and it proved extremely successful. The death rate for the patients he treated after surgery dropped from 50 percent to only 15 percent. Over the course of the next five years, he developed the technique of spraying the operating room with a carbolic acid mist.

CHILDREN OF THIS INVENTION   Following up on the work of Lister, later studies showed that it wasn't really necessary to spray the air in the room as long as the wounds and surgical instruments were kept clean. Sterilizers were used to boil surgical instruments and disinfectants were used to wash down operating rooms. *Asepsis*, a technique in which doctors tried to keep all germs out of the operating room, replaced antisepsis in most hospitals, and modern medicine took a quantum leap forward!

PLASTICS

How many things can you list that are made of plastic? You'd better get a long sheet of paper because today it's hard to find things that don't have at least a small amount of plastic in them.

From the dishes we eat on to the clothes we wear, plastics are just about everywhere. Because they are lightweight, durable, and can be molded into virtually any shape, plastics have totally changed the world in which we live. It's hard to believe that 200 years ago, none of these miracle materials even existed.

Plastics belong to a group of materials called synthetic polymers because they are artificially made from long chains of molecules strung together. (The word *polymer* is Greek for "many parts.") The origin of modern plastics starts in the 1860s with the game of billiards and an amateur chemist named John Wesley Hyatt.

HOW IT WORKS   In the 1860s, billiard balls were made of ivory, a natural polymer found in the tusks of elephants and walruses. An American company, Phelan and Collander, was one of the larger makers of billiard balls and was having such a hard time getting enough ivory that they offered a prize of 10,000 dollars to the first person to come up with an acceptable replacement material.

John Wesley Hyatt, a printer from New York who had an interest in chemistry, took the challenge. He began mixing guncotton, the material that had replaced black powder in firearms, with other substances. After several failed experiments, Hyatt mixed guncotton with camphor and alcohol and heated it in a device that resembled a pressure cooker. Individuals with a better understanding of chemistry might not have tried this, fearing the material would explode; but instead of blowing up in his face, the mixture melted together to form a gooey compound that could be easily molded. Even better, when it cooled down, the material got very hard.

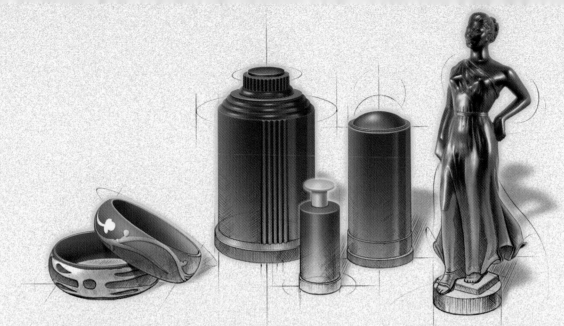

In 1872, Adolf von Baeyer mixed the chemicals phenol and formaldehyde together. He produced a thick mess that he saw no use for. Then, in the early 1900s, L. H. Baekeland recreated von Baeyer's experiments and created Bakelite. This unique material could be molded into objects of any shape including those shown here. Bakelite was used to make everything from costume jewelry and jewelry boxes to perfume containers and radio cases. It was responsible for turning the early plastic industry into a multimillion-dollar industry.

IMPACT   It's not known whether Hyatt won the prize, but in 1869 he patented celluloid, the first synthetic plastic. As it turned out, celluloid wasn't the ideal material for billiard balls because if two balls hit each other with enough force, they would actually explode! Instead, it wound up being used for making other things, like dental plates and camera film. From that day on, the modern plastic industry was off and running.

CHILDREN OF THIS INVENTION   While people like Adolf von Baeyer were working with synthetic dyes in Germany, an English scientist named Joseph Swan was busy trying to come up with a synthetic fiber that he could use as a long-lasting filament in the newly created incandescent lightbulb. In 1883, he invented a process for making a long, continuous fiber, but since it failed as a filament, he never developed it further. A few years later, Comte Hilaire de Chardonnet, a French inventor, was looking for a substitute for natural silk and stumbled upon Swan's discovery. Using Swan's process, he displayed *Chardonnet Silk* at the 1889 Paris exhibition, and the new fabric was a big hit. Today, we know this material as rayon, the first in a long line of synthetic fibers that not only make up our socks and pajamas, but also fishing line and medical stitches.

THE PHONOGRAPH

"At the sound of the beep, please leave a message." Who hasn't made a phone call and, instead of getting a live person, has gotten stuck talking to an answering machine? While it's both a blessing and a curse, today's modern voice-mail system with microprocessor and digital storage is just the latest in a very long line of sound-recording equipment that started in 1877 with the phonograph, invented by Thomas Alva Edison, "the wizard of Menlo Park." Over the years, Edison's life story has become a legend. More than 1,000 patents were issued in his name, but as it turns out, one of his most famous inventions, the phonograph, was one that he never even planned to market.

This early Edison phonograph, or "Ediphone," works strictly by mechanical vibrations. When a sound is made, vibrations in the air enter the device and hit a thin metal diaphragm that is attached to a thin needle or "stylus." As the diaphragm vibrates, it moves the stylus that cuts an up-and-down pattern onto a rotating wax-covered paper cylinder. This pattern on the cylinder exactly matches the vibration of the sound. To play it back, all you needed to do was place the stylus back at the beginning of the groove and turn the cylinder.

Unlike many inventions of the 1800s, there really wasn't a pressing need for a device to record sounds. If people wanted to preserve an important statement, or send someone a message, all they needed to do was write it down. If you wanted to hear music, you listened to a band, played an instrument, or sang a song. There were no pop stars to admire, and books were things to be read, not listened to on the car stereo while stuck in traffic.

HOW IT WORKS   The origin of the phonograph actually goes back to Edison's early years, when he worked as a telegrapher, a person who sent and received messages via Morse code on a telegraph line. In the late 1860s, he began working on a printing telegraph that could record messages on a waxed paper tape and transmit it later at high speeds. He noticed that if he pulled the bumpy paper tape past the spring of the "reader," it would make a sound much like a musical note. Adapting this idea, in 1876, he began developing a machine that an office worker could use to record letters on and have a secretary type later. What we call the dictaphone today started as Edison's first phonograph.

IMPACT   Edison's invention made an immediate impact on people at home who wanted to listen to prerecorded music. Edison began producing cylinder phonographs for the home market, but profits were weak. He was ready to give up production when, in 1887, Emile Berliner introduced the first flat-disk gramophone record. By mass-producing the flat records, Berliner's gramophone quickly cornered the market. While Edison fought a furious battle, he, too, finally gave in and produced a flat disk player, many of which are still in use today.

CHILDREN OF THIS INVENTION   In the end, a device that was first conceived to help get office work done in a more efficient manner turned out to be one of the most important popular inventions in the history of the world. Even though this early phonograph is a far cry from the modern recording equipment we use today, it set the stage for tape recorders and CD players.

The gramophone record offered a longer playing time than the cylinder, and because the needle vibrated side to side instead of up and down, it created far less distortion and produced a truer sound.

THE INCANDESCENT BULB

If you stop and ask someone who invented the electric lightbulb, chances are that most American citizens will tell you it was Thomas Edison. While it is true that Edison did invent the first practical lighting system, the electric light was invented 40 years before he was even born!

Because of the amount of power they consumed and the glare they produced, arc lamps, the first electric lights, never became popular for home use. By 1878, streetlights using this type of system were installed in Paris and a number of other European cities. To make an electric light truly effective, it would have to produce a continuous "soft" glow. The key was a Humphry Davy discovery called incandescence.

HOW IT WORKS   If you've ever looked inside a toaster when it's on, you've seen incandescence in action. Incandescence happens when a substance gets hot enough to glow. The wires inside a toaster glow red-hot because they only get up to around 400°F (184°C). If you were to heat them up to around 1000°F (480°C), they would have a bright white glow for a few seconds and then burn up.

In order to make a practical electric lamp, it was necessary to find a substance that could be used as a filament that would get hot enough to glow, but not burn. (The filament is the little wire inside the lamp that actually produces the light.) In 1860, when Thomas Edison was only 13 years old, Joseph Swan (the same person who invented rayon) was already working on the problem. He made a glass bulb, and in it he placed a filament made of carbonized paper. By pumping most of the air out of the bulb, he was able to get it to glow a little, but

The first working electric light was built by Sir Humphry Davy in 1807. Called an electric arc lamp, it looked a little like a continuous lightning bolt trapped in a glass ball. When the electricity was turned on, an extremely bright spark jumped across the rods producing a blinding white light.

still it wasn't close to being practical. Swan turned his attention to other matters, and in September 1878, Edison took up the task.

On December 18, 1878, Joseph Swan (who went back to working on the lightbulb) finally figured out the problem. By using a better vacuum pump, he was able to remove enough air from his bulb that it, too, stayed lit for several hours. He demonstrated a bulb similar to Edison's for the Chemical Society of Newcastle almost a year before Edison perfected his bulb, but because he had no means of mass-producing the lamp, Edison usually gets the credit for the invention.

IMPACT   Perhaps the greatest impact of the incandescent light was that you no longer had to work your day around the rising and setting of the sun. Edison went into immediate production and began construction of the first large-scale power distribution system in New York City. By September 1882, his Pearl Street station was lighting much of downtown New York City, and he was forever hailed as the "man who turned night into day!"

Edison was convinced that he would have a working lamp in less than a year. Unfortunately, the more he and his helpers worked at it, the more frustrated they became. Finally, after trying literally thousands of different filaments, he went back to carbonized silk thread. He lit this bulb on October 21, 1879, and it burned for 40 hours.

Edison's legacy goes way beyond the phonograph and the lightbulb because he completely changed the way inventing was done. One of the primary reasons that he was so productive was that unlike other inventors of his time, Edison surrounded himself with a group of talented individuals (his "boys," as he called them) to help him work out all the details of his inventions. In a sense, his greatest invention may have been the first industrial research lab!

CHILDREN OF THIS INVENTION   In order to make the lightbulb work, Edison also had to design sockets, switches, generators, and electric meters. Later, the incandescent lightbulb would be modified and turned into the first vacuum tube, the device that made radio and television possible.

chapter five

THE AGE

OF THE

ATOM

1887 - PRESENT

AS THE NINETEENTH CENTURY was drawing to a close, new inventions like the telephone, motorcar, diesel locomotive, and gramophone had made the world a "smaller" place. Using the power of electricity, people could communicate over long distances in a fraction of a second. People could now learn of important events in hours rather than weeks.

In the world of nutrition and medicine, innovations and discoveries were making it possible for people to live longer, healthier lives. Using a growing list of chemical fertilizers, farmers could produce far greater amounts of food from their fields, meaning fewer people were needed to support the growing population.

Near the turn of the century, it looked like things couldn't get much better. In scientific research labs throughout the world, fascinating new discoveries were being made that would revolutionize our technological development. Strange new phenomena such as radiation and electromagnetic waves were being detected, and after centuries of trying, scientists were about to unlock the secrets of the atom.

RADIO BROADCASTING

Today, radio broadcasts bring us everything from the latest news to the Top 40 hits. With so many different types of programs available, it's hard to believe that radio as we know it has been around for less than 100 years!

Technically speaking, radio was more of a discovery than an invention, and it began with early experiments with electrical current. In the mid-1860s, James Clerk Maxwell, an English physicist, tried to figure out why iron objects near telegraph lines were becoming magnetized. He proposed a theory which suggested that as electricity flows through the wire, it releases pulses of invisible energy called electromagnetic waves. Maxwell published his ideas in 1873, and in 1887, German scientist Heinrich Hertz proved him right. As it turns out, some of the energy pulses that Hertz discovered are what we now call radio waves. They probably would have remained a scientific curiosity if it had not been for Italian inventor Guglielmo Marconi, who was looking for a way to send telegraph messages without using wires.

HOW IT WORKS In 1894, 20-year-old Guglielmo Marconi read about what Hertz had done and thought of a way to use it in communication. He set up a lab at his father's estate near Bologna, Italy, and was able to send a signal over 1½ miles (2.4 km). The concept of "wireless telegraphy" had

Since 1897, Marconi worked on improving his transmitters, which allowed him to first send a signal across the English Channel in 1899 and then across the Atlantic Ocean in 1901.

become reality. Marconi formed his own company in 1897, and by 1900 it went international as the Marconi Wireless Telegraph Company.

Using a simple carbon microphone adapted from the telephone, Fessenden and his colleagues at the National Electric Signaling Company had figured out a way to place actual sounds on top of a constant "carrier signal" that could be transmitted. Fessenden called his system amplitude modulation, but we know it today as AM radio.

IMPACT   Because the wireless did not have to be connected via telegraph lines it was ideal for use at sea. Soon, ships from both the American and British navies were being equipped with this new device.

Wireless transmissions worked well for sending messages, but it still was not a radio broadcast. This changed on Christmas Eve of 1906, when Reginald Aubrey Fessenden scared the daylights out of wireless operators all over the East Coast of the United States. The silence in their headphones was suddenly broken by the sound of a violin and the spoken words of a Christmas poem coming right over the air! Most of them never realized that they had taken part in the first true radio broadcast.

Radio's impact on society cannot be overstated. In an instant, people all over the world can know of events as they are happening. Using radio, we can communicate with space probes on the edge of our solar system and talk to family and friends on our portable cell phones.

CHILDREN OF THIS INVENTION   Building on the work of radio pioneers, other inventors, like Philo T. Farnsworth in the United States and John Logie Baird in England, began experimenting with sending pictures over the air. With RCA and David Sarnoff taking the lead, television became a reality in 1939. Using a system developed by Vladimir Zworykin, RCA broadcast the first television transmission, showing President Franklin Roosevelt opening the New York World's Fair.

THE X RAY

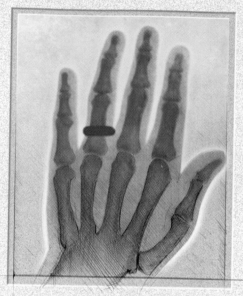

As a way of testing the X rays, Röntgen had his wife place her hand on a photographic plate, at which he fired the cathode-ray tube. The result was a clear picture of all the bones in her hand as well as the wedding ring on her finger.

At some time or another, just about everybody has gone to the doctor to have an X ray. It could be because you fell off a bike and hurt your leg, or maybe you had a sore tooth that the dentist needed to take a closer look at. Whatever the cause, X rays have become essential parts of modern medicine because they allow doctors to see what's happening inside the body without having to open you up and peek inside.

As with radio before it, the X ray was more of a discovery than an invention, but if it had not been for the keen eye of Wilhelm Conrad Röntgen, this important diagnostic tool might never have come about.

HOW IT WORKS   On November 8, 1895, a German physicist named Wilhelm Röntgen was experimenting with a device known as a cathode-ray tube when he noticed that across the room, a piece of paper that had been coated with the chemical barium platinocyanide began to glow whenever the tube was turned on.

IMPACT   Continuing his experiments with X rays, Röntgen found that they could pass right through skin and other soft tissue, but were stopped by dense material like bone. He also found that X rays would expose photographic plates just like light, even though you could not see them.

Within a few short years of Röntgen's discovery, the science of *radiography* rapidly expanded. Before X rays, the only way doctors could tell what was happening inside a patient was to open him or her up and take a look. Now, finding broken bones and foreign objects like bullets was simple. Röntgen received the Nobel Prize in Physics in 1901 for his work with X rays.

In 1897, an American doctor named William Cannon devised a way of seeing even soft tissue. By having patients drink a "milkshake" made with the element bismuth (later barium) and then x-raying them, he was able to find leaks in the human digestive tract. Today, X rays are quite routine, and scientists know that this mysterious form of radiation is simply another type of electromagnetic wave that, like visible light and radio waves, makes up a broad band of energy called the electromagnetic spectrum.

CHILDREN OF THIS INVENTION   Röntgen's discovery was so significant that in England, Sir Joseph John Thomson and his assistant, Ernest Rutherford, were determined to find out just how X rays worked. Repeating Röntgen's experiment, Thomson discovered that the mysterious cathode rays were nothing more than a stream of charged particles he called electrons. In 1897, he presented his first atomic theory of matter. Later, in 1913, Danish scientist Niels Bohr completed the first picture of the atom, the fundamental building block of all matter.

From a medical standpoint, this early work in X rays led to the development of other noninvasive, diagnostic tools like CAT scans and MRIs, giving modern medicine many opportunities to look inside us.

After trying many experiments with a cathode-ray tube, Wilhelm Röntgen came up with the idea that some unknown type of radiation was being generated by the tube. He found that this radiation could pass right through wood, paper, and even aluminum. Since he didn't have any idea what this new type of radiation was, he simply called them X rays.

THE AIRPLANE

Ever since people first saw birds in the sky, humans have had a desire to fly. For almost 3,000 years, people experimented with different types of flying machines, and with the exception of kites, they all had the same result: crash! It's no wonder that when Orville and Wilbur Wright rolled their Wright *Flyer* onto the

Ornithopters, or "birdlike flyers," never got off the ground because they were heavy. Unlike human bones, birds' bones are hollow, which make them strong but incredibly lightweight. Birds also have a great deal of muscle mass to get them going. Using a solid wooden frame, humans simply could not produce enough lift to get these devices off the ground.

beach at Kitty Hawk, North Carolina, on that cold December morning in 1903, they did it in secret. Like dozens of inventors before them, they expected the worst, but they were in for a great surprise. Their device stayed aloft, and the airplane was born. While the first flight of the Wright brothers is often considered the beginning of aviation, it really marks the end of many years of inventors' struggles to take wing.

HOW IT WORKS   The first true flying machines can be traced back to ancient China, where simple kites were used as signaling devices, in religious ceremonies, and for just plain fun! In Europe, inventors in Greek and Roman times tried desperately to mimic birds in designing a flying machine, but unfortunately, what comes naturally to birds is almost impossible for humans.

By the late 1700s, people had learned that instead of flapping like birds it was possible to fly by using the lift provided by a hot-air balloon. Balloons, which are called lighter-than-air craft, simply float. To fly, you still need wings. In 1792, Sir George Cayley, an English inventor who was obsessed with the idea of flight, began experimenting with a variety of "fixed-wing" craft which, as the name suggests, did not "flap" like the ornithopters. As early as 1804, he had built small-scale experimental models that worked fine. Cayley would have probably succeeded in getting a full-sized flying machine to work, except that he could not find a suitable engine to power it. As it was, in 1853, he built a fully manueverable glider that carried his trusty coachman more than 1,500 feet (460 m) across a valley near his home.

German inventor Otto Lilienthal made more than 2,000 flights in a variety of different gliders over the course of three years. He worked out most of the problems with steering, lift, and airfoil design. Wilbur and Orville Wright built on the work of Cayley and Lilienthal, to get off the ground.

IMPACT   Within a few short years, airplanes had become a crucial part of society. First, they were used to deliver the mail, and later, for military purposes. Today's airplanes move millions of people each year, making the world a much smaller place.

CHILDREN OF THIS INVENTION   While few planes in the air today look anything like the Wright *Flyer*, most of the design ideas remain the same. Although simple propeller-driven planes have given way to jet-powered craft, when the space shuttle lands, it comes in like a glider, just like the craft of George Cayley 200 years ago.

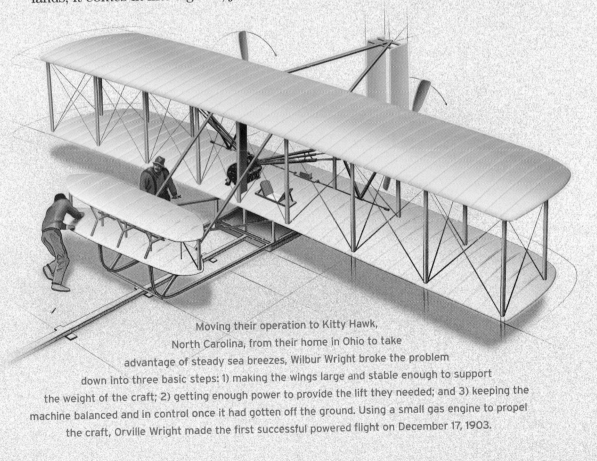

Moving their operation to Kitty Hawk, North Carolina, from their home in Ohio to take advantage of steady sea breezes, Wilbur Wright broke the problem down into three basic steps: 1) making the wings large and stable enough to support the weight of the craft; 2) getting enough power to provide the lift they needed; and 3) keeping the machine balanced and in control once it had gotten off the ground. Using a small gas engine to propel the craft, Orville Wright made the first successful powered flight on December 17, 1903.

THE ROCKET

Next time you're out and about on a clear, dark night, take a look up at the stars. If you're lucky, you might see a small light streak across the sky. If it's too high to be a plane and too slow to be a meteor, what you're seeing is probably one of the dozens of satellites orbiting Earth. Most people don't realize it, but these mechanical marvels not only help scientists predict the weather and monitor climatic changes, but they also make global telecommunications possible. While there is no question about how valuable satellites are to modern society, none of them would be up there if it weren't for the dream of Robert Goddard and the rockets he invented.

HOW IT WORKS   Unlike an airplane, which needs to get lift from its wings, rockets fly because of the enormous amount of thrust coming out of their back end. The origin of the rocket, like that of the airplane, can be traced to ancient China with the first use of fireworks and the discovery of gunpowder. These early rockets were simply hollow tubes packed with explosive powder. When they were set off, they blew up almost as often as they flew.

In the early 1800s, British arms expert William Congreve developed a solid propellant rocket that used a guidance stick and a central hollow core that helped the fuel burn more evenly. It was this device that produced the "rockets red glare" made famous in "The Star-Spangled Banner."

Throughout most of the nineteenth century, rockets were thought of as nothing more than self-propelled bombs, but in 1898, a Russian schoolteacher named Konstantin Tsilolkovsky came up with another idea: spaceflight! Tsilolkovsky did much research into the subject and published several papers on how rockets might be used in the future, but it was an American named Robert Goddard who actually got the job done.

In 1908, Goddard was a 26-year-old physics professor conducting research in rocketry at Clark University in Worcester, Massachusetts. He proved for the first time that a rocket didn't need to have air to push against and could easily fly through the vacuum of space. Goddard experimented with solid-fuel rockets, but realized that they were limited in how high they could go. He gave up the idea and developed the first liquid-fueled rocket motor. On March 16, 1926, Goddard successfully tested the first liquid-fueled rocket on his aunt Effie's farm in nearby Auburn.

IMPACT   In addition to his work with liquid-fuel engines, Goddard also built gyroscopic guidance and parachute recovery systems for his rockets. Unfortunately, he was never able to realize his dream of spaceflight; on August 10, 1945, Robert Goddard died of throat cancer. Because of his pioneering research, however, he will always be remembered as the "father of modern rocketry."

Based on Goddard's designs, other rocket pioneers like Hermann Oberth and Wernher von Braun in Germany were able to send rockets higher and farther than anyone had thought possible.

CHILDREN OF THIS INVENTION

Once rockets were available to take payloads out of Earth's atmosphere, there was a virtual explosion of developments, including satellites, space probes to other planets, orbiting space labs, and rockets to the moon!

Powered by a combination of liquid oxygen and gasoline, Goddard's first liquid-fuel rocket flew for only 2¹/₂ seconds traveling a total of 56 feet (17 m). Despite the small numbers, Goddard proved that his system could work.

ANTIBIOTICS

It happens to all of us from time to time. You get up in the morning and you just don't feel right. Your throat hurts, your ears ache, and you've got a fever. You take a trip to the doctor and discover that you have a case of strep throat. You don't have to worry, though, because the doctor hands you a piece of paper and on it is a prescription for a "magic bullet," an antibiotic that will knock the infection right out; in no time, you'll be up and running again. Today, antibiotics are one of the miracles of modern medicine, and while some scientists are beginning to think that in the long term they may be causing more harm than good, over the last half century they have helped millions of people survive serious infections.

HOW IT WORKS Antibiotics came about because of a series of discoveries in the early part of the twentieth century. Their use falls under a branch of medicine called chemotherapy, which was invented by a German doctor named Paul Ehrlich. Chemotherapy means "treating with chemicals," and it began in the 1800s with the discoveries of Louis Pasteur.

The biggest breakthrough in antibiotics happened by accident one day in 1928 in the lab of Sir Alexander Fleming, a British microbiologist. Fleming had been growing some staphylococci bacteria on a dish to study, when he noticed that a mold had also started to grow on the dish. Fleming noticed that the mold actually killed off some of the bacteria. He identified the mold as *Penicillium notatum*, a kind that frequently is found on old bread! In 1939, Howard Florey and Ernst Chain, working on a new idea called antibiosis, used Fleming's discovery and isolated the drug penicillin. This stained glass window from St. James Church in London celebrates the discovery.

Based on his work, people like Joseph Lister made great progress in cutting down the rate of infections through the use of antiseptics, but once a person got an infection, there was little a doctor could do but let it run its course and hope for the best.

In the early part of the twentieth century, doctors began experimenting with different chemical compounds, with mixed results. Some of these treatments not only killed the germs, but the patients, too. In 1906, Paul Ehrlich discovered Salvarsan, a synthetic chemical that killed the microbe responsible for the disease syphilis. Ehrlich was so excited that he called the drug a "magic bullet," and he came up with the term "chemotherapy" to describe the style of treatment.

IMPACT   To this day, penicillin is still one of the most effective antibiotics, and because of its wide range of uses, it, too, is frequently called the "magic bullet."

Over the past 50 years, many additional antibiotics have been discovered, and their use has skyrocketed. As with most good things, there is also a downside. While antibiotics kill off most of the invading germs, they often leave behind a few that are resistant to the drug. Over time, these "super germs" multiply, so that the next time they invade, the antibiotic is less effective, or may not work at all.

CHILDREN OF THIS INVENTION

Today, the use of chemotherapy has spread to many other areas of medicine besides infections. The use of specialized chemicals, along with radiation, has allowed doctors to combat not only invading bacteria, but also many forms of cancer as well.

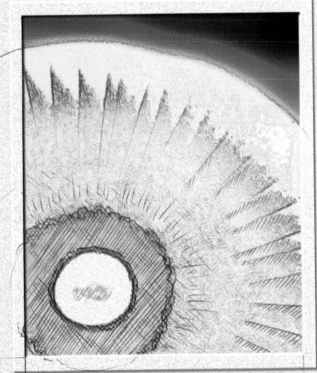

This is the mold that Fleming found growing in his dish. It is called *Penicillium chrysogenum*.

THE NUCLEAR REACTOR

During the course of human history, no single development has offered as much promise and generated as much debate as nuclear power. A list of the names of the people involved in the study of atomic energy reads like a Who's Who of twentieth-century science. People like Marie Curie, Albert Einstein, Enrico Fermi, and dozens of other great minds have all had a hand in it. While atomic energy is more of a discovery than an invention, two major inventions—the atomic bomb and the nuclear reactor—have come about as a direct result of its development.

HOW IT WORKS   Unlike chemical reactions that happen between atoms, nuclear reactions happen because of changes in the nucleus of an atom. Some elements like radium and uranium literally lose pieces of their nucleus and change over time into new elements. In this process, they release energy in the form of radioactivity, which can then be used as a power source for making electricity, or bombs. Radioactivity was discovered by Antoine-Henri Becquerel and Marie and Pierre Curie in the 1890s, for which they received the Nobel Prize in Physics.

Over the next 30 years, many scientists in Europe expanded the study of radioactivity, eventually working out what exactly was going on. In the early

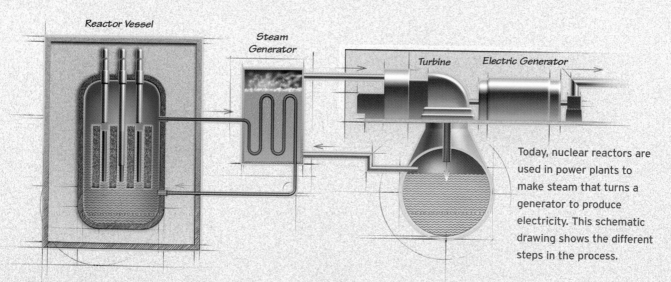

Reactor Vessel

Steam Generator

Turbine   Electric Generator

Today, nuclear reactors are used in power plants to make steam that turns a generator to produce electricity. This schematic drawing shows the different steps in the process.

1930s, Adolf Hitler rose to power in Germany, and because of the beliefs of the Nazi Party, many of the European scientists involved in the research in Germany and Italy defected to the United States. One of those scientists was Italian physicist Enrico Fermi.

Fermi thought that he could use the high-energy particles released from one natural nuclear reaction to trigger other reactions in a series of controlled steps. In so doing, he believed he could set up a "chain reaction" that would continuously release a tremendous amount of energy. He and his team set to work on the problem, and by December 2, 1942, they had constructed the first nuclear reactor at the University of Chicago.

On July 16, 1945, the first nuclear bomb, code-named "Trinity," was exploded in the desert of New Mexico. On August 6, a similar bomb called "Little Boy" (top), estimated to have the force of 20,000 tons of dynamite, was exploded over the Japanese city of Hiroshima. Three days later, a second bomb known as "Fat Man" (bottom), which was made from the element plutonium 239, was dropped on the city of Nagasaki.

IMPACT   While the initial idea of Fermi's work was to come up with a virtually unlimited power source to propel society into the future, World War II created other, more pressing needs. In the summer of 1939, a group of scientists, including Fermi and Albert Einstein, approached President Franklin Roosevelt to discuss the possibility of using an uncontrolled fission reaction to make a nuclear bomb. Eventually, bombs were dropped on Japan. While these weapons caused massive amounts of death and destruction, they did succeed in bringing the war to a rapid close.

CHILDREN OF THIS INVENTION   Fermi's research led to the development of a variety of peacetime nuclear reactors, which have been used to generate electric power for cities, ships, and even spacecraft. The problem is that nuclear power comes with a price. No matter how safe they appear, nuclear reactors always pose the threat of a deadly leak.

In addition, no one has yet come up with a way to dispose permanently of the highly toxic waste that they generate. Since this material stays radioactive for thousands of years, the solution has to be a long-term one!

THE COMPUTER

Today computers are just about everywhere, from the ignition system of our cars to the tuners in our digital radios. Millions of us use personal computers in our homes for everything from video games to home finances. This very book was written on one!

Although computers are thought of as modern, high-tech devices, they actually date back to 1822, when Charles Babbage, an English mathematician, was looking for an easier way to count numbers.

HOW IT WORKS To understand how the computer was invented, we must first define exactly what a computer is. Simply stated, it's a programmable device that helps solve problems by processing information, following a series of instructions. In 1812, Babbage came up with the idea of using punched cards to input data into an "analytical engine." He built a series of calculators leading to

The first electric computer was Hollerith's electric tabulating machine. His machines became a success both in the United States and Europe, and in 1896, he set up the world-famous Tabulating Machine Company. Never heard of it? Well that's probably because in 1924 its name changed to International Business Machines (IBM).

his prototype machine. Unfortunately, Babbage's groundbreaking ideas couldn't be turned into reality due to the limits of the equipment of the day.

Picking up on some of Babbage's ideas, an American inventor named Herman Hollerith was determined to come up with a way of automatically tabulating census data. Hollerith had worked on the 1880 U.S. census and found it to be very time-consuming. By the 1890 census, he had a working device which used punched cards to input data via an electric card reader.

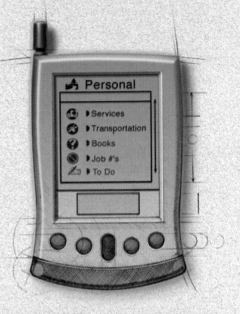

Today's portable personal computers use microprocessors to pack as much computing power in the palm of your hand as the ENIAC computer had—and it took up an entire building!

IMPACT Through the early part of the twentieth century, electric calculators flourished, but they had their limits. Small improvements were made along the way, but clearly mechanical systems were a dead end. For a device to be really fast and versatile, it would have to use the same type of electronic tubes that made radio and television possible. In 1939, American physicist and mathematician John Atanasoff built a prototype of an electromechanical digital computer. His model was the first ever to use vacuum tubes to do computations, and the only thing keeping it from being a modern computer was the lack of programming.

To say that computers have changed society would be a gross understatement. There is hardly any part of our daily lives that isn't affected by a computer in some way, shape, or form. But as sophisticated as computers are, they still need people to program them.

CHILDREN OF THIS INVENTION The first truly digital, multipurpose, fully electronic computer, designed by J. Presper Eckert and John W. Mauchly, was unveiled at the University of Pennsylvania in 1946. Called ENIAC (Electronic Numerical Integrator and Computer), the system contained over 18,000 tubes, and used more than 100 kilowatts of electricity (that's 1,000 100-watt lightbulbs on at the same time!), but it was a thousand times faster than anything before it. In a few short years, this, too, would change, because at that same time, in another part of the United States, the transistor was being invented.

TRANSISTORS AND IC CHIPS

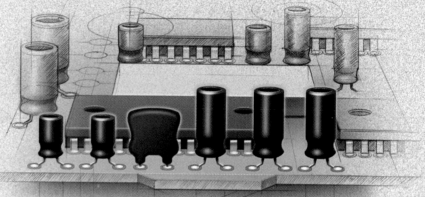

In the 1940s, you needed a small building to hold a computer with the power of ENIAC. Today, that same computing power can be found in many desktop machines. This was because most of the circuits that operated early computers used vacuum tubes, which were big, bulky, and very inefficient. While vacuum tubes made

These early transistors were made from the semiconductor silicon. As the name suggests, a semiconductor is neither an insulator nor a conductor, but something in between. William Shockley discovered that by adding impurities to silicon chips, he could make them switch electrical current on and off, and even have the current change direction. Soon, transistors were replacing vacuum tubes, which were not only big and bulky but gave off a tremendous amount of heat.

electronic devices like computers, television, and radio possible, they had their limits. To make a device truly practical and portable, something was needed that worked like a tube, but used less power and was more compact.

This was the dream of three engineers working at Bell Labs: John Bardeen, Walter H. Brattain, and William B. Shockley. It was their brainchild that would propel the world into the digital revolution when, in 1947, they introduced the first transistor.

HOW IT WORKS   Transistors are basically electronic switches that can do almost anything that a vacuum tube can do, plus a whole lot more. A transistor can be made smaller than the point of a pencil, and because it has no filament, it consumes far less power than a tube and never gets hot. Also important, transistors aren't made of glass, so when you drop them, they don't break as easily.

The idea of the transistor came about as a result of the need during World War II to pack as much equipment into as little space as possible. Radios, radar, and other electronic gear had to be made portable, but with tubes, it was tough going. Scientists had known for some time that when it came to electricity, most materials fell into one of two groups: conductors like copper and iron, which let electricity flow freely through them, and insulators like rubber and glass, which stop the flow of electricity. The Bell Lab group had developed a third type of material, the semiconductor.

In 1947, Bardeen, Brattain, and Shockley introduced the first transistor, and the electronic industry exploded. For their efforts, the three were awarded the Nobel Prize in Physics in 1956. But the real payoff was yet to come.

IMPACT   Because transistors can be made small, the idea of packing a great many of them onto a tiny surface was really inviting. Beginning in the early 1950s, engineers began experimenting with integrated circuits or ICs, tiny chips of silicon with transistors and other solid-state components etched right onto the surface. Electronically, these microchips are really quite simple. They are nothing more than a collection of wires and switches, but because a chip the size of a shirt button can hold as many as a half million components, they are incredibly powerful!

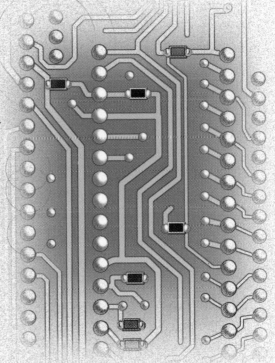

CHILDREN OF THIS INVENTION

Today, integrated circuits are in virtually every type of electronic equipment. They have not only reduced the size of many devices, but the price, too, because they cost so little to make. Because of ICs, not only have we been able to send space probes off to the far reaches of the solar system, but doctors can now implant tiny computers in the human body to keep us running right.

Microchips like this one can be broken down into a few different groups. Memory chips are used in computers and other devices to store information. Clock chips run things like electronic watches and help computers run according to a certain timing sequences. The most important IC is the microprocessor, a computer that is as small as your thumbnail. These are often inserted into other devices and act as the nerve center.

THE LASER

The final invention covered in this book is the laser, and it's only fitting because like the hand ax a half-million years ago, the laser is today's most effective cutting tool. In addition, low-powered lasers can be used to "read" digital codes by scanning them with pulses of light, which operate almost instantaneously.

The word *laser* is an acronym standing for *l*ight *a*mplification by *s*timulated *e*mission of *r*adiation, and even though it wasn't fully invented until 1960, the idea for it was proposed by none other than Albert Einstein in 1917.

A ruby laser works because chromium atoms in a ruby rod are stimulated by bursts of light coming from a coil surrounding it. This "flash tube" causes the chromium atoms in the ruby to become excited, and when they return back to their "normal" state, they give off light in the form of an energy bundle called a photon. This photon sets off a chain reaction, and as more and more photons travel through the rod, they build up an intense beam of light, which is focused by two curved mirrors at either end of the ruby rod.

HOW IT WORKS   Einstein had been working with light for some time when an idea hit him. He suggested that if you could get light of just the right frequency to hit an excited atom and stimulate it further, that atom would give back its excess energy in the form of light when it returned to its original unexcited state.

Einstein never did much with the concept (probably because the equipment to build such a device had yet to be invented), but in 1953, American physicist Charles Townes, working at Columbia University, picked up on the idea. Instead of using visible light, he built a device that used a different form of electromagnetic radiation called the microwave and he called it the *maser*, an acronym for *m*icrowave *a*mplification by *s*timulated *e*mission of *r*adiation.

Working at the Hughes Research Labs, Theodore Maiman, a 32-year-old graduate of Stanford University, heard about the maser and began doing some of his own experiments. Maiman made a number of very important design changes that greatly improved the efficiency of Townes's maser, but his real interest was in using visible light. Using a ruby rod, Maiman was able to build the first successful laser in 1960.

IMPACT   Despite what most people think, a laser's power is not in the total amount of energy it gives out, but in the concentration of that energy on a small surface. Because laser light is monochromatic (one color) and coherent (all waves vibrating in the same direction), it can be used in many applications. Large industrial lasers are used for cutting steel, while smaller ones are used by doctors in surgery. Because their power level is adjustable, lasers can be used today in hundreds of different devices from computer printers to supermarket scanners.

CHILDREN OF THIS INVENTION   Laser technology is still in its infancy, and like the computer before it, there is no telling what it might spawn. Soon, security systems will use a laser to read the retina of your eye like an optical fingerprint, and the next phone call you make will probably be carried by a beam of laser light!

Today, lasers are at the heart of most fiber-optic communications systems and many security systems, and they are even used as sights on surveying equipment. Perhaps the most enjoyable use of lasers is in entertainment—they are used to read compact music discs and CD-ROMs.

LOOKING AHEAD

AS WE CONCLUDE THIS BOOK, our journey through human invention and technology has spanned almost two million years. Along the way, we've seen how people of the past learned to use the materials around them to make their world a better place. Over the years, inventions have gotten more complex, but the one thing that has stayed the same is the inventive spirit that makes humans special.

At the present rate of development, it's hard to imagine where we will be in 10 years, much less a century from now. Yet with all our "improvements," it's important to remember that technology has a dark side, too. While the invention of the internal combustion engine has given us the freedom to roam, it has also created environmental problems like air pollution and global warming. The development of nuclear power offers the promise of inexpensive electricity, but it has also produced highly destructive weapons that, in the wrong hands, could virtually wipe out life on our planet.

Every invention, from the simple hand ax to the laser, has given humans the ability to change the world around them. In the past, most scientists and inventors only worried about whether or not they *could* do something; in the future, the key will be thinking first about whether or not they *should* do it!

Hopefully, in reading this book about inventions of the past, you might become inspired to become an inventor, too. The key to becoming a successful inventor is imagination. Remember, too, you're never too young to start inventing. Philo T. Farnsworth was only fourteen years old when he designed the circuit for the first electronic television, and Thomas Edison began conducting his experiments before the age of 10! The most important part of inventing is being able to see something that needs improving, and then taking action to make the change. Whether it's building a better mousetrap, or solving the world's energy crisis, necessity has been and will continue to be the mother of invention!

BIBLIOGRAPHY

53 ½ Things That Changed the World and Some That Didn't!, by David West and Steve Parker, The Millbrook Press, 1992

Invention and Technology, by Milton Lomask, Scribner's, 1991

Inventors and Inventions, by Michael Jeffries, Smithmark, 1992

The Picture History of Great Inventors, by Gillian Clements, Alfred A. Knopf Books, 1994

Steven Caney's Invention Book, by Steven Caney, Workman Publishing, 1985

Super Invention Fair Projects, by Dr. Zee Knapp, Lowell House, 2000

Technology in the Ancient World, by Henry Hodges, Barnes and Noble, 1970

The Way Things Work, by David Macaulay, Houghton Mifflin Company, 1988

WEB SITES

Camp Invention

http://www.invent.org/camp_invention/camp/main.htm

If you've ever thought about being an inventor or you just like to mess around with "stuff," then Camp Invention is for you. Sponsored by the National Inventors Hall of Fame, this one-week summer day camp is hosted in dozens of different schools and museums around the country. Geared toward students in grades 2–6, it's a place where your imagination is the only limit!

How Things Work

http://howthingswork.virginia.edu/

This site is like a radio call-in show where people get to ask Physics Professor Louis Bloomfield of the University of Virginia specific questions about how common devices work. In addition to being able to ask your own questions, there are literally hundreds of questions already posted on the site.

Invention and Design

http://jefferson.village.virginia.edu/~meg3c/id/id_home.html

This site is designed to promote a better understanding of the principles of invention and design. It contains numerous resources, hands-on modules, and an extensive index.

The Invention Dimension

http://web.mit.edu/invent/

This site, sponsored by MIT, offers a wealth of information on both present-day and historical inventors. In addition, it provides links to many other invention-related sites.

National Inventors Hall of Fame

http://www.invent.org/

If you're looking for information on a famous inventor, this is the place for you. There are dozens of short biographies indexed by both the inventor's name as well as the invention. In addition, there are links to many other invention-related sites.

INVENTION CONTESTS

Craftsman/NSTA Young Inventors Awards Program

http://www.nsta.org/programs.craftsman.asp

This contest challenges kids to use their own creativity along with science and technology to invent or modify a tool. Sponsored by the National Science Teachers Association, the contest is open to students in grades 2–8 who live in the United States or a U.S. territory. For more information log on, or write:

Craftsman/NSTA Young Inventors Awards Program
National Science Teachers Association
1840 Wilson Boulevard
Arlington, VA 22201-3000

ExploraVision

http://www.toshiba.com/tai/exploravision

This competition, sponsored by Toshiba Corp., is designed for U.S. or Canadian students in grades K–12. It's purpose is to encourage kids to combine their imaginations with science to explore a vision of future technology. Kids work in a research-and-development team along with an adult mentor to project how a certain technology will evolve in the future.

INDEX

Adj mer, 41
Agriculture, 16–17, 22, 30, 40–41
Airplane, 79, 94–95
Alloys, 39
Alphabetic principle, 31
Anaximander, 44–45
Anesthesia, 68–69
Animals, domestication of, 17
Antibiotics, 59, 98–99
Antiseptics, 59, 80–81
Architecture, 14, 19
Art, prehistoric, 14–15
Atanasoff, John, 103
Axle, 26–27

Babbage, Charles, 102–103
Baekeland, L. H., 83
Baeyer, Adolf von, 83
Baird, John Logie, 91
Bakelite, 83
Bardeen, John, 104–105
Battery, 66–67
Becquerel, Antoine-Henri, 100
Bell, Alexander Graham, 75
Bell Lab group, 104–105
Benz, Karl, 79
Berliner, Emile, 85
Bi Sheng, 50
Black powder, 54–55
Boats, 24–25
Bohr, Niels, 93
Bookmaking, 49, 50–51
Brady, Mathew, 71
Brattain, Walter H., 104–105
Brick making, 18–19

Cai Lun, 48–49
Camera obscura, 70–71
Canal systems, 40–41
Cannon, William, 93
Cathode-ray tube, 92–93
Cato, 76

Cave paintings, 14
Cayley, Sir George, 94–95
Chemical revolution, 54–55
Cities, 18–19
Clark, William, 69
Clocks, 52–53
Clothing, 20–21
Coins, 36–37
Compass, 56–57
Computer, 102–103
Congreve, William, 96
Cooke, William, 74–75
Copernicus, Nicolaus, 61
Crops, 16–17, 22, 76–77
Cuneiform writing, 30, 48
Curie, Marie and Pierre, 100

Daguerre, Louis, 71
Davy, Humphry, 68, 76–77, 86
de Chardonnet, Comte Hilaire, 83
de Rochas, Alphonse Beau, 79
Decimal system, 32
Dugout canoes, 24–25

Eastman, George, 71
Eckert, J. Presper, 103
Edison, Thomas Alva, 75, 84–85,
    86–87, 108
Ehrlich, Paul, 98–99
Einstein, Albert, 100, 101, 106
Electric light, 86–87
Electric motor, 67, 72–73
Electricity, 65, 66–67
Electromagnet, 67, 73
ENIAC, 103, 104
Explosives, 55

Fabric making, 20–21
Faraday, Michael, 73, 74
Farnsworth, Philo T., 91, 108
Fermi, Enrico, 100–101
Fertile Crescent, 17

Fertilizers, chemical, 76–77
Fessenden, Reginald Aubrey, 91
Firearms, 55
Fishing, 22–23
Fleming, Sir Alexander, 98
Fulton, Robert, 63

Galilei, Galileo 60–61
Galvani, Luigi, 66–67
Gears, 43
Goddard, Robert, 96–97
Grains, 16–17
Greenlees, James, 81
Gunpowder, 54–55
Gutenberg (Gensefleisch),
    Johannes, 51

Hammurabi, Code of, 41
Hand ax, 10–11, 13
Heliograph, 71
Henry, Joseph, 73
Hertz, Heinrich, 90
Hieroglyphics, 30–31
Hollerith, Herman, 103
Hooke, Robert, 58–59
Hospital fever, 80–81
Hughes Research Labs, 107
Hunting, 12–13
Huygens, Christian, 53, 79
Hyatt, John Wesley, 82–83

IC chips, 105
Incandescent bulb, 86–87
Industrial Revolution, 63, 65
Internal combustion engine,
    78–79
Irrigation systems, 17, 40–41

Janssen, Hans and Zacharias, 58

Kilns, 23

Labor, division of, 17, 29
Laser, 106–107
Lever, 13
Liebig's law, 77
Lilienthal, Otto, 95
Lippershay, Hans, 60–61
Lister, Joseph, 80–81, 99
Long, Crawford, 69

Magnetic compass, 56–57
Maiman, Theodore, 107
Maps, 29, 44–45
Marconi, Guglielo, 90–91
Mathematics, 19, 32–33
Mauchly, John W., 103
Maxwell, James Clerk, 90
Measurement, 29, 34–35
Metallurgy, 38–39
Microbiology, 58
Microscope, 58–59
Mills, 42–43
Monetary system, 36–37
Money, 29, 35, 36–37
Morse, Samuel F. B., 75
Morton, William, 69
Motorcar, first, 79

Natural fibers, 20–21
Navigation, 53
Newcomen, Thomas, 62
Newcomen engine, 63
Niepce, Joseph Nicéphore, 71
Nitrous oxide, 68–69
Nuclear reactor, 100–101
Number systems, 32–33

Oberth, Hermann, 97
Oersted, Hans Christian, 72
Otto, Nikolaus, 78–79

Paintings, 15
Papermaking, 48–49
Papyrus scrolls, 48
Pasteur, Louis, 59, 81
Penicillium chrysogenum, 99
Phonograph, 84–85
Phonographic symbols, 31

Photography, 70–71
Pictographs, 15
Place-value system, 32
Plastics, 77, 82–83
Plows, 16
Poles, law of, 72–73
Pottery, 14, 22–23
Pressure-flaking technique, 11
Printing, 49, 50–51
Ptolemaeus, Claudius, 45
Pyramids, Egyptian, 19

Radiation, 89
Radio broadcasting, 75, 90–91
Radioactivity, 100–101
Radiography, 92–93
Rafts, 24–25
River valley regions, 18
Roads, 27
Rocket, 55, 96–97
Rollers, 26–27
Röntgen, Wilhelm Conrad, 92–93
Royal master cubit, 35
Rutherford, Ernest, 93

Sails, 25
Salvarsan, 99
Sarnoff, David, 91
Savery, Thomas, 62
Schilling, Baron, 74
Schulze, J. H., 70–71
Sculptures, prehistoric, 14–15
Shockley, William B., 104–105
Smelting, 38–39
Sound-recording equipment,
    84–85
Spear, 11, 12–13
Spear-thrower, 13
Standards, measurement, 34–35
Stars, 44–45
Steam engine, 62–63
Stephenson, George, 63
Stock ticker, 75
Sumerian cuneiform, 30
Swan, Joseph, 83, 86–87
Symington, William, 63
Synthetic fibers, 83

Tanning, 20
Telegraph, 67, 74–75
Telephone, 67, 75
Telescope, 60–61
Terra Amata huts, 18
Textiles, 20–21
Thomson, Sir Joseph John, 93
Thread, 21
Tools, metal, 38–39
Townes, Charles, 106
Trade, 17, 21, 29, 36–37
Trade centers, 19
Transistors, 104–105
Trevithick, Richard, 63
Tsiolkovsky, Konstantin, 96–97

van Leeuwenhoek, Antonie,
    58–59
Venus figures, 14
Vitruvius, 43
Volta, Alessandro, 66–67
von Baeyer, Adolf, 83
von Braun, Wernher, 97
von Liebig, Justus, 76–77

Warfare, 19, 55
Water-use rules, 41
Waterways, 24
Waterwheels, 42–43
Watt, James, 62–63
Weaving, 20
Wedge, 10
Weight standards, 35
Wheatstone, Charles, 74–75
Wheel, 26–27
Wireless telegraphy, 90–91
Wright brothers, 79, 94–95
Writing, 14, 29, 30–31, 49
Wu Ching Tsao, 54

X rays, 92–93

Zero, 33
Zworykin, Vladimir, 91